THE BILLINGS ENIGMA

By the same author

George Pell: Defender of the Faith Down Under
Enid Blyton at Old Thatch
The Power of 100: One Hundred Women Who have Shaped Australia

As Editor

Be Not Afraid: Collected Writings
Golden Priest, Wooden Chalice
Test Everything: Hold Fast to What is Good
Brisbane Queensland: Towards the 21st Century
Queensland, Australia: Opportunity & Enterprise
Upon This Rock: the First 50 years of St. Peters Lutheran College
Mr Waffles and Plum Pudding
Textiles at the Cutting Edge

THE Billings enigma

Tess Livingstone

with a Foreword by Cardinal George Pell

connorcourt
PUBLISHING

Published in 2013 by Connor Court Publishing Pty Ltd

Copyright © WOOMB International Ltd 2013

ALL RIGHTS RESERVED. This book contains material protected under International and Federal Copyright Laws and Treaties. Any unauthorised reprint or use of this material is prohibited. No part of this book may be reproduced or transmitted in any form or by any means, electronic or mechanical, including photocopying, recording, or by any information storage and retrieval system without express written permission from the publisher.

Connor Court Publishing Pty Ltd.
PO Box 1
Ballan, VIC 3342
sales@connorcourt.com
www.connorcourt.com

ISBN: 978-1-922168-375 (pbk.)

Cover Design: Ian James

Printed in Australia

CONTENTS

FOREWORD.. v

INTRODUCTION... viii

1. EVELYN'S STORY.. 1

2. JOHN'S STORY... 15

3. THE LONGEST THREE MONTHS IN HISTORY........ 31

4. THE TIMES THEY WERE A CHANGIN'................... 51

5. BUILDING MOMENTUM.. 69

6. THE RESEARCH STACKS UP.................................. 87

7. COAL, IRON ORE AND NATURAL FAMILY PLANNING....... 101

8. NOW AND INTO THE FUTURE................................ 115

9. BOM AND THE SENSUS FIDELIUM........................ 129

EPILOGUE.. 153

ACKNOWLEDGEMENTS... 161

Foreword

The Billings Enigma is an important story which needed to be written for posterity and for us today as the world confronts an increasing population on some continents and an accelerating demographic decline in Russia, Japan and much of Europe. The story is an important Catholic story, but noteworthy too because it records an extraordinary humanitarian contribution in many countries; especially in what we used to call Communist China, with its notorious one-child policy and abortion enforcers. God writes straight in crooked lines we are told, and this was never more apparent than in the repeated invitations the Billings received to lecture and work in China.

I have followed these issues for some decades, but I learnt a lot from these pages. The invention of the contraceptive pill produced a continuing cultural revolution and the long delayed response of *Humanae Vitae* by Pope Paul VI in 1968 spelling out the traditional Catholic teaching against artificial contraception was rejected by many Catholics, while its prophetic message of the consequences of a contraceptive mentality have been exemplified over the years and into the present.

Some ironies are apparent, such as Germaine Greer insisting that the abortifacient qualities of some contraceptive pills should be known by the women who use them. A Catholic education is never completely wasted! It is interesting too that the Billings method in the Western world is now used extensively to enhance conception as older mothers, sometimes after years of using the pill, struggle to conceive.

Older readers too will be surprised and reassured to hear that the married couple is a "radiant icon of Trinitarian love", so that a proper approach to sexuality recommends the "nuptial mysticism" of married sexual activity.

Christians are separated from our increasingly secular world by their attitudes to love, justice, forgiveness and the obligations towards new life which non-Christians do not always share. No couple has done more for pro-life strategies than the Billings.

The author notices that Dr John and Dr Evelyn Billings are better known outside Australia than at home. This small, quality book will help remedy this imbalance.

George Cardinal Pell
Archbishop of Sydney

DEDICATION

This book is dedicated to Mother M. Xavier McMonagle OSB and the Tyburn sisters whose prayers mean so much to so many

Introduction

The Billings Enigma is a story of contradictions. It is about an Australian couple from Melbourne, the parents of nine children, who created the most reliable method yet devised of natural family planning -- or in secular language, natural birth control, that is used by an estimated 50 million couples worldwide.

It is the story of how and why their discovery, known as the Billings Ovulation Method (BOM), which accords with the Catholic Church's moral teaching, has been more successful in the world's largest non-Christian nation, China, than anywhere else.

And it is also the story of how the Method's widest use in Australia and other developed nations is no longer directed towards preventing pregnancy but facilitating it, as increasing numbers of infertile couples of all faiths and none, struggling to conceive the children they long for, turn to the BOM as a last resort.

Central to this story's twists and turns are two extraordinary main characters – a sports-loving, highly academic boy from Hawthorn in Melbourne's leafy eastern suburbs and a book-loving country girl from Jerilderie in southern New South Wales. John Billings and Evelyn Thomas caught each other's eye over a dead body in the University of Melbourne anatomy rooms during a dissection class in 1938. As Rosalind said in *As You Like It*, John and Evelyn "no sooner met but they looked, no sooner looked but they loved" and "made a pair of stairs to marriage" that spanned more than six decades. He asked her to a ball, she accepted, and from that night onwards their lives unfolded together. She became a specialist paediatrician, he was one of the founders of the Australian Association of Neurologists.

Drs Billings and Billings are probably better known in China and the Vatican than in Australia, although they are respected and liked among a significant section of the Catholic Church and the wider Australian community. They were honoured to be named as Members of the Order of Australia in 1991. Their vision and tireless work, which came at a price for themselves and their family, has touched millions of lives. And the veracity of their research has been proven time and again in empirical trials.

Readers who believe in the providence of God might also understand this story as an example of how Divine Grace unfolds in extraordinary ways.

Lyn as Dux of St Michael's Church of England Grammar School

1
Evelyn's Story

The strongest loves transcend our earthly lives to eternal life, and so it was for the legendary Drs Evelyn and John Billings. At age 94 in early 2012, Evelyn's material world was the tree-lined avenues of Kew in Melbourne's east. It was not far from where John was born in Burton Avenue, Hawthorn, on 5 March 1918, where he attended school and was Dux of Xavier College in 1935. He and Evelyn were thrilled when their grandson, Paul Reynolds, repeated his grandfather's achievement at Xavier in 2006.

Evelyn Livingston Thomas, or Lyn, as her family and friends called her, was also born in the last year of the Great War, on 8 February, and grew up in prime Merino grazing country in the NSW southern Riverina town of Jerilderie. As well as being the birthplace of Sir John Monash, Jerilderie was made famous by Ned Kelly and his gang who held up the local bank and telegraph offices in 1879 and where Kelly penned his famous Jerilderie letter. Lyn's second name, Livingston, was her mother's surname.

Lyn, her brother Henry, who was five years older, and her parents, Henry and Evelyn Thomas, lived in the town, where her father was shire engineer and the family worshipped at the Church of England. Her mother was Australian-born and her father originally a New Zealander. Their ancestors were Scottish,

Welsh and Cornish. The family's property, *Bungoonah,* was about 10km outside the town, where Lyn often rode her beloved Bonny, a bay horse with a white blaze.

She and Henry were pupils of the two-teacher Jerilderie public school, where Lyn excelled at stories and poetry. Her love of the Australian bush ballads of Banjo Paterson and Henry Lawson stayed with her for eight decades. Science did not particularly interest her, although led by Henry on hikes and bush picnics she shared her brother's interest in birds and wildlife. Lyn learned piano, from "a dear old Mercy nun, Sister Casimir" – the first Catholic she got to know well.

"It was a very happy childhood," she said emphatically, although it was sometimes lonely because the age gap between herself and Henry meant they were "more like two single only children", especially when Henry was boarding in Melbourne to attend Melbourne Grammar and later Haileybury College. Her long, solitary days riding Bonny were a factor in Lyn's desire to have a large family herself. "I would have loved to have had a sister. Later on I really wanted to have a daughter." Lyn graduated from Jerilderie Public School at the end of 1930 as Dux.

Like many country children of her era, Lyn left home at age 12 in 1931 to board, living with her maternal grandmother, Genefor Livingston, at Middle Park in Melbourne. Genefor's late husband was Thomas Livingston, a former teacher, newspaper editor and businessman who was a Victorian MLA for Gippsland South from 1902 to 1922. Evelyn travelled by tram and train each day from Genefor's home to St Michael's Grammar School, St Kilda, which was then run by the Community of the Sisters of the Church, an Anglican teaching order. Lyn enjoyed school but missed home and the country. English remained her favourite subject.

At the start of her final year at St Michael's in 1936, Lyn's father, Henry Thomas, planted the idea of her becoming a doctor. For a man of his era, when daughters' career plans did not concern too many fathers and in many cases were actively discouraged, sometimes with a heavy hand, Henry Thomas showed admirable ambition for his daughter and a real appreciation of her potential. Lyn was already studying advanced Maths, and to realise her ambition she began attending Chemistry and Physics classes. She graduated from St Michael's as Dux.

In contrast to today's competitive race for university places, Lyn recalls that entering the medical course at the University of Melbourne was "not hard", although she found the first two years "extremely tough" as she caught up on the years of science she had not studied at school. She lived on campus, at Janet Clarke Hall, which then, like now, is a leading academic residential college with an elegant, red brick late Victorian facade. It is affiliated with the Anglican Church and its most celebrated graduates include 2010 Nobel Prize winner and cancer researcher Professor Elizabeth Blackburn, former CSIRO chairman Professor Adrienne Clarke and author Helen Garner.

The college prides itself on its record of providing women with equal access and equal opportunity since 1886, when it was endowed by benefactor Janet Clarke. While meeting the challenge of bringing her scientific knowledge up to scratch, the young Lyn Thomas thrived in the College's supportive and intellectually stimulating atmosphere. Despite the fact she was one of only 20 women in a class of 100 male students beginning their medical studies in 1937, she was seemingly unaware that such choices were exceptional in her era.

Lyn with fellow student and good friend Helen Morris in academic gowns, 1942

Endowed with a solid, quiet confidence, Lyn Billings did not see the need for feminism to help other women achieve their goals. If there were any gender barriers in her path she either ignored them or did not notice. From the outset of the course she always intended to be doctor as well as a mother and was prepared to work as hard as needed. A few months into the course she knew: "I had found my life's work." The speciality of Paediatrics, caring for children, appealed and "I also knew that I would like to have a few children."

It was early in 1938, the year Hitler's forces marched into Czechoslovakia and Neville Chamberlain declared "peace in our time" that second-year medical student Evelyn Thomas, looking over a row of dead bodies in the dissecting room in the Department of Anatomy, caught the eye of a third-year student who was the prosector (practical demonstrator) for the class. As Lyn told ABC television's *Compass* in 2009: "I was well and truly alive so that was an advantage I had. I knew he was very bright. And he was very kind, and gentlemanly – all those things that a girl really needs in the man that she chooses." John invited her to a ball at Newman College, where he lived, an invitation she accepted readily.

She quickly realised she had met her match – in every sense. "We both had our professions, a strong bond. I knew from the outset that we would be very happy and we were." Six decades later, their family and close associates remained struck by the intensity and affection of their bond. Watching them on speaking platforms their colleagues noticed how their eyes would light up watching and listening to each other, how enraptured they were with every word of each other's presentations and the seamless unity between them. Five years after John's death in April 2007 Lyn often dreamed that he was still with her, and she sometimes awoke thinking "I must tell him this or that." To state the obvious, that she missed him dearly, was to understate how close she continued to feel to him. After a bad fall laid her low shortly before Christmas 2012 and she was admitted to Caritas Christi Hospice in Kew fully conscious she told visitors she had "a very important meeting". She didn't want to keep John waiting.

Wedding portrait, 1943

As students, their romance had strengthened as their courses advanced. Her engagement ring, as the couple's eldest daughter Eve Provan told a packed congregation at St Patrick's Cathedral in a eulogy for her father, was bought with the proceeds of a medical school prize he won. The couple were married a few months after Lyn's graduation, when she was a resident doctor at the Royal Children's Hospital, Melbourne. *The Argus* newspaper reported on Monday, 8 February 1943:

> Bride Wears Mother's Veil. The marriage of Capt John Billings, AAMC, youngest son of Mr and Mrs R. B. Billings, Whitehorse Rd, Balwyn, and Dr Evelyn Thomas, only daughter of Mr and Mrs H. W. Thomas, Bungoonah, Jerilderie, NSW, was celebrated on Saturday at Newman College Chapel by Rev Father T. Johnston. The bride, who wore her mother's coronet tulle veil with her bridal gown of Alencon lace, was given away by her father. Sub- Lt Bob O'Hara. RANVR, was best man.[1]

Their honeymoon was a few days holiday at the beaches along the Great Ocean Road, west of Melbourne. Theirs was a meeting not only of hearts and minds but of faith. By the time of her wedding Lyn, who had been well grounded in the Christian faith as an Anglican, decided to take on her husband's religion. She also, "under sufferance", took on his support for the Hawks, the Hawthorn VFL team.

Both sets of parents were supportive of the match, although some relatives on both sides, as well as wider acquaintances in those days of intense sectarianism, frowned upon the "other side's" religion. Lyn, however, was unfazed. "He believed that the Catholic Church had the authority and had the truth… He couldn't give it up…no way could he give that faith up. Well I wasn't giving anything up. I was taking on a whole heap more…"[2]

After years of Anglican services and scripture classes, Lyn had no trouble accepting the teachings of the Catholic Church, including transubstantiation, the Papacy, and the Immaculate Conception. Given her fundamental beliefs, Lyn felt it made sense that she, her husband and future children should worship together. Both wanted a large family. At the same time, it never occurred to her that she would do anything but press ahead with her medical work.

In many ways, chatting to Lyn Billings in her 90s was like chatting to a woman half her age. Her intellect remained prodigious. In late 2011 her scientific understanding and explanation of "black holes" in the universe astounded Bishop Peter Elliott, a distinguished scholar and old friend who quickly found himself out of his depth on the subject. Lyn had also lived the challenge of so many modern women – balancing career and family – and finding there are never enough hours in the day. Younger women who've lived the "having it all" dream – or nightmare – probably relate to her more easily than some older women whose lives ran along more clearly defined paths of being either housewives or career women, but rarely both. Like many women, she also shared in caring for her ageing parents and her parents-in-law.

In 1947 the Drs Billings travelled to London, where John took up a Nuffield Fellowship to study neurology at the National Hospital in Queen's Square. Lyn studied at Great Ormond Street Children's Hospital in Bloomsbury, an international centre of excellence supported over the years, among others, by Charles Dickens and J.M. Barrie, who bequeathed the rights of *Peter Pan* to the hospital. During her time there Lyn earned a Diploma of Child Health from London University. A keen reader and history student, Lyn loved London where the couple lived in Bayswater, near Hyde Park. Because England remained in the grip of wartime rationing, John and Lyn decided to leave their children, Eve and Jimmy, behind in Australia. The children lived with their grandparents at Jerilderie.

Lyn and John on their way to Buckingham Palace for a garden party

It was a grim time in London, brightened for the Drs Billings by an invitation to a Buckingham House Garden Party for Nuffield Fellows. The black and white image of the smartly-dressed young couple remained one of Lyn's favourite photographs. Eve observed during her father's eulogy: "It must have been an agonizing time of separation despite the fact that we were superbly cared for … I remember their homecoming from England and being most impressed by my 'very pretty' mother and 'really tall' father and perhaps not so impressed by a noisy new brother! Peter was born in England."

By the age of 30 in 1948, Evelyn Billings had taken on a new faith, qualified as a doctor in Melbourne and as a medical specialist in London and had three children. She, like John, saw private patients at 55 Collins Street, Melbourne, although unlike him she worked professionally part-time. As well as her work as a paediatrician and later promoting the Billings Ovulation Method, Lyn "cooked, cleaned, shopped and sewed – it was a very busy life." So busy that she occasionally fell asleep saying the Rosary with John at night. With admirable frankness, their children admit that they were "too naughty and too noisy" to be included – a sign, perhaps, that their parents were probably more gentle and less rigid than many of their era who would have pressed the point.

Lyn remembered that she often managed to beat the pressures of the clock, making time to sew a clown suit for her son John one Christmas. But at times the family felt the pressure, in the same way that children of high-achieving parents do today. A series of housekeepers helped keep the household running, but the children's happiest homecomings after school were on the days Lyn was home. The growing family eventually included another six children – David born in 1950, twins Helen and Ruth (whom Eve felt were an answer to her prayers for a sister) born in 1951, Joan in 1954, John in 1956 and Catherine, the youngest in the family who was adopted by John and Lyn shortly after her birth in 1959.

Her professional career also continued apace. In 1969 the *Medical Journal of Australia* published her study of 478 neonates at risk from difficult and anoxic births (a birth where the child is deprived of oxygen). The following year, Lyn began 13 years in a part-time teaching position in the Anatomy School of Melbourne University as a Senior Demonstrator in Embryology and Histology.

In an interview for Mothers Day 2012 in *Kairos,* Melbourne's Catholic magazine, Lyn acknowledged the role played by her older children, especially Eve: "The big ones used to look after the little ones – Eve was the eldest, so she had a special load to carry. If they couldn't find me, they'd go to Eve to find out things. They used to take notice of what she said; they all loved her."

During one of their parents' first overseas trips to Rome in 1961, the children's grandmothers, Evelyn Thomas and Elizabeth Billings, teamed up to hold the fort. From all reports the older women, one intensely Catholic and the other Anglican rubbed along reasonably well. Looking after the children, however, who ranged in age from two to 18, was akin to "managing kittens coming out of a box" as Lyn described it. During that trip one of the boys managed to set fire to his bedroom – fortunately the damage was contained.

The family's happiest, most relaxed times were on holiday.

In the early years they went to Mordialloc, on Port Phillip Bay, setting off after Christmas with the girls travelling in one car with the cat and the boys in the other with the dog. They stayed in beach huts. Later the family bought a country retreat, a property on Mt Toolebewong outside Healesville, in Victoria's scenic Yarra Valley, and built a comfortable house that accommodated all of them. John especially enjoyed the fireplaces in the living room and his office. Always a smart dresser, his children, to

Lyn with baby Eve in the 1940s

their amusement, recall him out chopping wood and even using a chainsaw – wearing his usual tie. For decades, the property was a haven of relaxation free of work commitments for Evelyn and John, their children and friends, sons and daughters-in-law and grandchildren, who relished their all-too-rare time with "Honey and Pop."

Lyn with 'Mac' mid-70s

1. http://trove.nla.gov.au/ndp/del/article/11348822
2. *Compass* with Geraldine Doogue. 26 April 2009. http://www.abc.net.au/compass/s2542293.htm

John James Billings

2
John's Story

John Billings, whom many remember as a charming, kind and exceptionally talented man, who had a stubborn streak on occasions, was a sportsman, scholar and soldier before he became one of Australia's leading neurologists. A cradle Catholic, he and his brother, Bob, and two sisters, Mary and Betty spent a happy childhood in Hawthorn in Melbourne's eastern suburbs, the area that remained John's home district for 89 years. His father, Robert, was an accountant and his mother, Elizabeth, kept house. In addition to his academic success at St Joseph's Primary School and Xavier College, John excelled at cricket and football. On the cricket pitch, his best performance for Xavier was against Scotch College, taking 6 for 20 off 17 overs and scoring 54 runs in the same match.

At University he captained the Newman XI and played Aussie rules football for the college and for the Uni Blacks. His high marks early in his medical course prompted the lecturers to select him, as a third year student, to help as a demonstrator in the Anatomy Department for students in the year behind his, which was how he spotted a vivacious, dark-eyed young woman over a row of bodies. For him the attraction was instant, he later told Lyn, who admitted that initially she was "more interested in the dead body." Of 102 medical students in John's class, he graduated second in 1941, with high honours. If one of the greatest gifts a man can give his children is to love their mother, John excelled with flying colours. In fact, it is clear that the couple adored each other from the outset and their love and affection increased with the years.

After living and working as a resident medical officer at St Vincent's Hospital, Melbourne, at the same time Evelyn lived and worked at the Queen Victoria Hospital across town, John enlisted in the AIF early in 1943 to serve with the Australian Army Medical Corps. He was initially sent to Sydney for a course of instruction on tropical diseases. And he married Evelyn while on leave.

After returning to Australia in October 1944 from Papua New Guinea John served in Australian army hospitals before

John seated front row left with Xavier First XI cricket team

his discharge on 21 October 1946. John's son David told those gathered for his father's funeral on 4 April 2007 that John was proud of his army service, not just because he was part of the force defending Australia, "but to him there was a moral surety in the notion of defence itself. This was to be a constant in his life, defence of a moral principle, defence of the innocent."

A peaceful man by nature, John found the army a challenge, although in late years he looked back on the experience with some fondness. As David recalled: "He was very proud of his success as a doctor. He boasted to his friends at home that in treating the tropical illnesses of malaria, scrub typhus, dengue fever and dysentery, no one died. He spoke with sadness about the condition known then as 'war neurosis'.

"He was treating Japanese Prisoners of War. He told me shocking stories about Japanese POWs being thrown out of aeroplanes above the jungles near Lae to scare a remaining few into giving information about positions and supplies.

"He did not want me to think that atrocities were perpetrated only by the Japanese. He would surely have spoken out against this type of immorality and perhaps suffered himself for it. I can't be sure about this, but he did spend a large part of his life defending moral principles and the virtues associated with justice. He *was* brave."

The Royal Australian College of Physicians records that "John published on amoebiasis in Papua New Guinea and also on viral encephalitis", tended to repatriated former prisoners-of-war and served at the Pulmonary Diseases Hospital in Bonegilla, Victoria and Melbourne's Repatriation Hospital at Heidelberg.[1]

Being away with the AAMC he did not see Eve, his first child, until she was 11 months old. For a devoted family man, and hundreds of thousands like him, it was a major sacrifice, something that Eve and his subsequent children became aware

John during basic training at Puckapunyal

of in later life. "Separation from us was something that worried Dad a great deal and the conflict between the demands of his work and spending time with his family was a constant challenge for him. I knew nothing of that conflict. It was always just so good when he came home!"

Professionally, 1946 was a significant year for John, who earned his MD (Doctorate of Medicine), membership of the Royal Australasian College of Physicians and the Nuffield Fellowship, which allowed him to develop his interest in neurology in London. Returning to Melbourne in 1948, he convinced authorities at St Vincent's Hospital of the importance of neurology and was appointed head of the specialty at the hospital. In a tribute to his colleague written for the RACP, Dr Peter Bladin recalled:

> John tackled the task with his usual vigour and persistence. In 1950 he obtained his own clinical unit complete with inpatient beds and outpatient clinic.
>
> He was Head of the Department of Neurology at St Vincent's until he retired in 1983. He served on the Medical Advisory Council of St Vincent's Hospital for a decade, and he was Associate Dean (Clinical) of its clinical school from 1973 to 1983. In addition he was appointed neurological consultant to the Eye and Ear Hospital Melbourne, and also to the Peter McCallum Cancer Hospital and the Infectious Diseases Hospital, Fairfield. He served on the Council of the Royal Australasian College of Physicians, from 1952 to 1970, and represented the College on the NHMRC, for a period chairing many of its committees. This very significant contribution was recognized by the establishment of the John Billings Scholarship ...

His pioneering contributions to the establishment of the clinical specialty of neurology in Australia are of great historical significance.

Proud father of Eve and Jimmy

As a clinician John had a compendious knowledge of both general medicine and of clinical neurology. He built a reputation for his consultative skills and his problem solving in this area. His reputation as a clinical teacher was legendary; both undergraduates and those seeking postgraduate achievement sought his help and his Saturday morning ward rounds quickly became a 'must attend' feature of medical studies at St Vincent's Hospital.'[2]

Dr Bladin recalled John as a "delight; his warm personality and slightly shy manner combined to put one at ease immediately." He was also a willing mentor to junior colleagues – in fact, a born teacher who relished and excelled in the role. David recalls his father's indignation when, at the age of 65, he had to step down as the Dean of the Clinical School at St Vincent's when "he was just getting warmed up."

In *The Flowering of a Waratah: a History of Australian Neurology and of the Australian Association of Neurologists*, published in 2000, retired Professor Mervyn Eadie of the University of Queensland noted that John Billings was the youngest of the eight originating members of the Australian Association of Neurologists. Eadie recalled John Billings as "seemingly ageless" over his long service at St Vincent's working in collaboration with neurosurgeon Dr Frank Morgan, while younger doctors came and went.

Professor Eadie recalled:

John Billings as a neurologist was a clinician and not a researcher, though he published a number of articles on neurological phenomenological topics during his career e.g., paraplegia following chest surgery (Billings and

Robertson 1955). His professional life spanned almost the first half-century of the existence of Australian clinical neurology and his activities played a significant part in the growth of the speciality. He also played a distinguished role in the wider Australian medical scene. At an age when most men, if they had survived as long, would have felt justified in leisurely and perhaps contemplative inactivity John Billings has remained energetic and vigorous, his mental capabilities undimmed, his physical appearance largely unchanged and his strong sense of duty towards society undiminished by the passing of the years.[3]

As well as being an ideal day for teaching his students because of his lighter patient schedule, Saturday was also the day John's children looked forward to in their father's busy life. John would sometimes put on old clothes and spend the day in the garden, listening to the football on the radio. Those days are Eve's happiest memories of her father. "They were absolute bliss. It didn't happen often but it happened." John and Evelyn were the antithesis of today's stereotypical over-driving, over-protective "hothouse parents".

John's Saturdays started much earlier, when he would rise at dawn and travel to Melbourne's Victoria Market and do the family's weekly fruit and vegetable shopping before travelling to the hospital. He befriended the Chinese greengrocers at the markets where he found he could buy top quality produce to feed a family of 11 more economically than at the local supermarkets.

David Billings also recalled that his parents were always "terribly busy" which made the time they had together as a family extremely precious. The family foundations were "rock solid".

To use a modern term, John and Evelyn, from all accounts, were true soul mates. David recalled they were "very good parents, nurturing, affectionate and interested in what we were doing at school and accessible, despite their busy lives." His father was usually at work in his home office by 7.30 am. David remembers him as a gentle man, with an acute consideration for the needs of others. But like any father of nine children (or far fewer) in the house, he could occasionally "lose it". Despite his long working days, he usually made it home for dinner in the evenings and was involved in his children's lives. He was immensely proud of them all. He would say: "We have 9 children you know – Eve, Jimmy, Peter, David, Helen, Ruth, Joan, John and Catherine" reciting the list slowly, savouring each name. As Eve recalls he was "quite undaunted by the possibility that some recipients of this information might not be totally riveted!"

At weekends, David occasionally went with his father and grandfather to watch Hawthorn play, and sometimes John watched his sons play for Xavier. Mostly, however, the boys walked the short distance to school by themselves for Saturday games, or travelled by tram to other schools or went with a school coach to more distant games in Geelong. Living so close to Xavier and Genazzano Colleges, where the Billings girls attended school was a distinct advantage for such a busy family, as was living close to a tramline. When David was 14, his father, to keep fit, took on Australian Rules Football umpiring at Xavier for several seasons.

John also loved music, particularly choral music and enjoyed many concerts given by the Melbourne Chorale. Eve, who later taught music professionally at Genazzano College, remembered: "We were all encouraged to learn music. He used to love listening to us all practising – piano in one room, violin in another, someone singing in the bathroom – 'besides" he would say, 'when you can hear what they're doing you know they're being good!'"

In the wider community, he was a leading player in the establishment of Right to Life movements in Australia and the St Vincent's Bioethics Centre. As his longstanding colleague Dr Joe Santamaria said at his Requiem Mass, John Billings personified Benedict XVI's view that "all human activities should be an opportunity and an occasion for the growth of individuals and society, an opening to develop personal talents which must be valued and placed at the orderly service of the common good, in a spirit of justice and solidarity. For believers, the ultimate aim of work is the building of the Kingdom of God."

One of the Billings' saddest family times occurred in 1994 when their daughter Ruth, Helen's twin, by then a mother of five children, died at age 43 after a period of ill health from complications following surgery. Both John and Evelyn had feared for her health and for them, the nightmare of her sudden deterioration and death, surrounded by her own family and her siblings, was worsened by the fact that they were in Rome and stranded as they struggled to find seats home at such short notice. Decades later, the memories continued to bring Evelyn to tears.

Courageous and tenacious in his beliefs, John was admired by his family and friends for what Eve termed "his acute sense of justice" and his fearlessness in defending his faith. As his children grew to adulthood they also appreciated his understanding and respect for their individuality. "To his everlasting credit he accepted, albeit I am sure with much difficulty, that differences of belief would occur in his family and that we would not all live strictly according to his belief." Commenting on that one day he told Eve "you just have to love them and pray for them." His children and grandchildren, Eve says, have inherited many of his values and his commitment to humanity, with most of them entering "caring" professions. "Above all they have learnt the power of love." Eve, Jimmy, David, Helen and Joan became teachers, with David also working as a musician, composer and arranger. Peter is a clinical psychologist, Ruth was a nurse – the profession for which Joan has retrained – John is a lawyer and Catherine an aged care therapist. Evelyn's living room was full of family photos of her 39 grandchildren and 31 great grandchildren.

Sadly, as someone who treated neurological diseases in what remains a largely unchartered field of medical research, John Billings succumbed to the ravages of dementia, a cruel process that tested Lyn and their family to the limits as its ravages almost broke their hearts.

At times the pain and anguish felt unbearable as the family drew closer together than ever. Before John's death on Palm Sunday, 1 April 2007, Eve sensed that "he seemed to know what was happening and he certainly knew we were there. He had moments of lucidity which were pure gold."

John's death was reported by Neil Wilson in the *Herald Sun* newspaper on 3 April 2007:

ONE of Australia's most famous and controversial contributors to the study of fertility has died in Melbourne. Dr John Billings pioneered the scientific study of natural methods of contraception in the 1950s. His work was supported by the Catholic Church and the World Health Organisation.

The Billings family planning method changed the lives of generations of women.

It also helped women improve their chances of becoming pregnant by observing the timing of ovulation.

Dr Billings, 89, died late on Sunday at a Richmond aged care centre from complications of a long illness.

Supporters in bioethics and research said yesterday the official adoption of the Billings ovulation method in China

Lyn and John with all nine of their grown up children

after 1996 meant he had helped many millions of women.

Bioethicist Nicholas Tonti-Filippini, a co-founder with Dr Billings of the St Vincent's Bioethics Centre, said: "John Billings is so well known outside this country because of the impact of his work, particularly in the developing world. "With his wife, Lyn, they have made an unbelievable contribution to the welfare of women, liberating so many from having to rely on other methods of contraception."

Preaching the homily at his funeral in Holy Week, John's close friend, Monsignor (now Bishop) Peter Elliott recalled an encounter with John years before, at a retreat house near the Yarra River that defined John's character and his love for children:

> During a break, I walked out on to the lawn and there was Dr John Billings surrounded by little children. First they ran to him and soon they were running with him towards us, with all the gleeful freedom that only little ones know. That instant, bathed in Australian sunlight, was for me a foretaste of God's great day when this man would be welcomed into the Kingdom of heaven by multitudes of the Holy Innocents of our human race, those little ones to whom the Kingdom belongs.
>
> Now, at least in terms of our earthly time, that day has come. In Melbourne's noble cathedral we offer the redeeming Sacrifice of Jesus Christ, this Holy Mass for a man so many of us know and love. I cannot put that in the past tense, "a man we knew and loved", for John Billings has entered eternal life. While we struggle forward here in "shadowlands" he is now more alive than we are. He is in the refining mercy of God's eternal present moment. That is what we believe when we look to the risen Lord Jesus.

As Bishop Elliott said, while each person is unique and unrepeatable, certain people in history respond to the vocation of Baptism in a way that is distinctive, rare in its virtuous quality and fruitfulness. In one lifetime, such people, with God's grace, accomplish what would take 10 lifetimes for most other people. "John was such a man."

1. (http://www.racp.edu.au/page/library/college-roll/college-roll-detail&id=579
2. Ibid
3. Mervyn J. Eadie, *The Flowering of a Waratah: A History of Australian Neurology and of the Australian Association of Neurologists* (John Libbey and Company, Sydney) 2000

*National Health & Medical Research Council, 1970,
John Billings seated fourth from left*

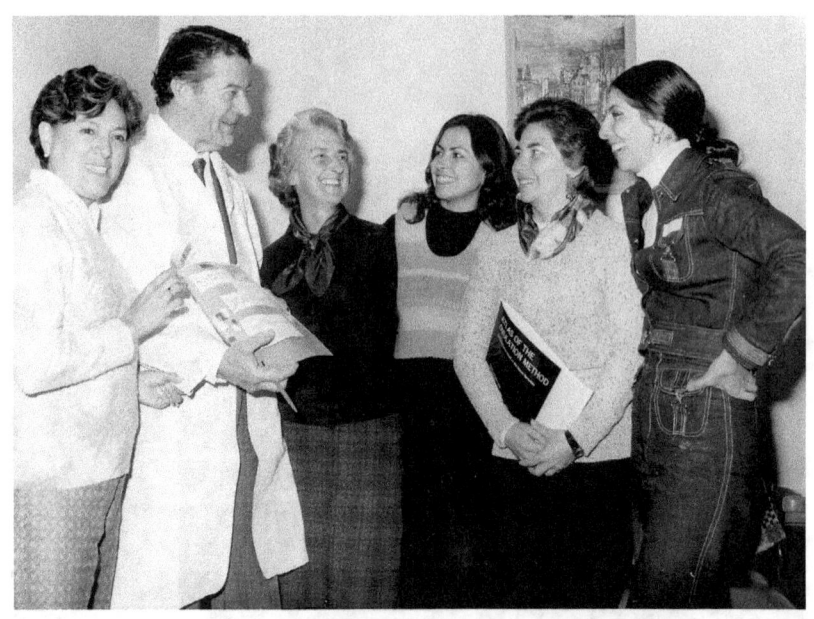
Drs Billings with Australian teachers of the Method, 1974

3
The Longest Three Months in History

From the outset of their marriage, John and Lyn had both wanted a large family and had the means to care for and educate nine children. The issue of birth control, and the Catholic Church's long-standing opposition to artificial birth control, barely crossed their radar. For many others, however, the problems posed by that teaching posed an enormous moral and practical dilemma. Contraception was far from reliable, anyway, but less reliable still was the so-called "rhythm method" or "Vatican roulette" tolerated by the Church, which only worked for women whose monthly cycles were sufficiently regular to make periodic abstinence effective. Years earlier, Dr Kaysaku Ogino in Japan and Dr Herman Knaus in Austria had each demonstrated that the next menstrual period followed ovulation by about two weeks, but what women needed urgently was an accurate marker of ovulation.

By 1953, Lyn and John, both aged 35, were enjoying building their medical careers. John's teaching load was also significant, six of their children had been born and were at primary school and at home. The family was firmly established in Kew. Both John and Evelyn were active in the Guild of St Luke, a Catholic doctors' group that in those days, as their fellow member and friend Dr Joe Santamaria recalls, was

... a vibrant association of Catholic doctors who were interested in the Church's teachings on moral theology and medical ethics. It was a period when Pope Pius XI and Pope Pius XII wrote on Christian marriage, birth control, abortion, euthanasia and the philosophy of Catholic hospitals. It was also a period when the Code of Nuremberg (a set of ethics for human research and experimentation) was enunciated and the Declarations of Geneva and Helsinki were formulated. The United Nations promulgated its Declaration of Human Rights in 1948 and Margaret Sanger launched the forerunner of International Planned Parenthood. It was a vital period in the history of health care as the medical profession tried to distance itself from the atrocities of the Second World War and the Catholic Church articulated its magisterial statements on marriage, fertility regulation and the impending battle with the culture of death.

A young Melbourne priest, Father Maurice Catarinich, whom Archbishop Daniel Mannix had recently appointed to run Melbourne's Catholic Marriage Guidance Bureau, was worried because the birth of too many children had left many poorer Catholic families under severe stress in overcrowded homes, barely able to feed their children. Fr Catarinich, who participated in meetings of the guild of St Luke, asked John Billings to help by way of providing more effective natural family planning. John told Father Catarinich that he would devote three months, part time, to the task and see the couples one evening a week. Dr Santamaria believes Fr Catarinich chose John because he understood the teachings of the Church and would tackle the problem with "a scientific mind, moulded by an intuitive understanding of conjugal love and responsible parenthood."

In a letter to California's Secretary of State Kevin Shelley in 2004 John recalled that, after the interviews with the couples began one night a week,

> [I]t was not very long before I was impressed both by the seriousness of the medical problems and the resolution of the couples that they would not under any circumstances accept advice to act in a way that was contrary to their religious faith. Then they might say, 'Can you help us?' All I could say in reply at that time was, 'I will try'.
>
> Evelyn and I had not discussed the subject of contraception before or since we were married because we were quite sure that each of us wanted a big family. We had learned the basic principles of the Rhythm Method in the medical course at the University, and also had acquired a moderate knowledge of the Temperature Method. I knew the weaknesses of these two methods and realised that a better method must be found to help these courageous people to overcome their problems.
>
> I began to spend time in medical libraries at the University and at St Vincent's Hospital, searching in the first instance for a clue that could suggest a new idea that would be acceptable and lead to a satisfactory natural method of regulating births, one that was as good as and preferably better than any other method, natural or otherwise, that had so far been discovered.
>
> It was notable at this time that a lot of attention was being paid to the activity of the cervix of the uterus. I was attracted to statements going back to the 19th century in London, England, where Dr W.T. Smith in 1855 and Dr J.M. Sims in 1868 reported that vaginal discharge of a fluid nature was observed by some women at the fertile time in

the cycle. With Fr Catarinich supplying diagrams which he devised to help the women record accurate observations, we told the couples that they could engage in intercourse after menstruation had ceased, until the beginning of this discharge from the vagina, and then resume intercourse three days after the discharge had ceased. It was necessary to restrict the acts of intercourse to alternate days before the commencement of the fertile phase, so that a woman would not confuse seminal fluid with cervical mucus. From the fourth day after the end of the mucus pattern defining the fertile phase, intercourse is available every day without the possibility of pregnancy. There were no pregnancies following that advice.

The Ovulation Method, as it was originally named, was on its way. Evelyn recalled that information about a likely physiologic marker indicating the few days when a woman was at her most fertile, regardless of her cycle, had been noted in the mid-Victoria era.

But nobody had thought of asking women about it, so that's what John did. That was the brilliant stroke, really, talking to women and asking them to identify it. Up until then, it had been mainly men working in that field, but when women got into the act they were able to show that this was verifiable throughout the female population.

That was the exciting thing, it was really quite extraordinary, and when it was put to women that this was something they could do themselves, they were encouraged to try to do that.

John Billings progressed the work part-time, in addition to his responsibilities as a neurologist, and in 1962, New Zealand-born endocrinologist Professor James Brown, transferred from Edinburgh to the Department of Obstetrics and Gynaecology at the Royal Women's Hospital and University of Melbourne. Professor Brown, who had developed a test for measuring estrogen levels, was a leading global scientist on ovarian and pituitary hormones.

John wrote in 2004:

> "I visited him at the Royal Women's Hospital soon after his arrival and he very willingly agreed to my request to conduct daily measurements of the ovarian hormones in a group of women of reproductive age, in order to determine whether or not what we had concluded from our clinical studies of days of fertility in a fertile menstrual cycle was correct. His laboratory techniques confirmed all the conclusions we had made."

Professor Brown concluded that the Billings Method contained in its rules an effective, natural solution for preventing pregnancy in whatever phase of her reproductive life a woman needed it. By that point, many of the women who visited John at his clinic were also being urged by their general practitioners to take the newly-available contraceptive Pill.

In 2010, retired US obstetrician/gynaecologist Charles W. Norris, a graduate of Georgetown University Medical School in 1957, wrote an account of the early days of the development of the Method in a tribute to John and Lyn Billings, who were awarded the President's Medal in 2005 by Georgetown University.

Dr Norris's article, published in *The Linacre Quarterly* by the Catholic Medical Association, recalled that Professor Brown

Professor Jim Brown, Dr John Billings, Dr Joe Santamaria, colleagues from the early days

conducted 750,000 hormonal assays (investigative procedures in a laboratory) to prove the correctness of Dr Billings' observations.

John Billings published his first book, *The Ovulation Method*, in 1964 and it was while proofreading the work in 1963 that Dr Evelyn Billings became fascinated with the research. She joined the team, taking on patients regarded as "hard cases" who had stumped the all-male team. After interviewing and working with the women, Lyn asked her husband: "Where did you say were all these hard cases?" Dr Joe Santamaria recalls that the "hard cases" were women who had trouble identifying the fertile phase of their cycles and Lyn "discovered that the cause of the problem was the male teachers who lacked the linguistic sensitivity necessary for asking the right questions ... Her feminine instincts discovered that women are the best teachers", a point that was to become vital in the spread of the Ovulation Method throughout the world. The "difficult cases", which had comprised about 30 per cent of those seeking help, quickly dwindled.

Lyn studied almost 100 premenopausal women between 1965 and 1969, research that helped define the Basic Infertile Pattern and opened up the Method to women who were breastfeeding and those with long or irregular cycles. The development of a monthly chart, complete with coloured stamps, some with symbols, simplified the teaching process and ensured that for those in the know, tedious daily temperature recordings lost their relevance.

As Dr Norris recorded:

> "So Lyn was on board. Other problems she addressed with considerable success were those of the breastfeeding woman when ovulation could be delayed for months, and also the months and years prior to the onset of menopause, when one's cycles become much more irregular and ovulation less frequent.
>
> "It was due to her efforts that it became apparent that women, experiencing the mucus symptom physiologic marker themselves, would make the best teachers of the ovulation method. As the mucus symptom is prospective and temperature readings retrospective, the team concluded that the thermometer was not necessary."[1]

Others in the natural family planning world disagreed, however, which marked the beginning of what could flippantly be called "the natural family planning wars", which have been no less intense and hard fought at times than the "history wars" or the "literacy wars".

Confronted with resistance from advocates of the thermometer method, John and Evelyn Billings forged their own path. As early as 1972, they moved away from the "official" Catholic Family Planning establishment in Melbourne due to disagreements over the Billings advocacy of use of the mucus marker alone, without temperature monitoring as backup. They continued to enjoy the support of Melbourne's Catholic Archbishop of the time, Cardinal James Knox, and set up an independent centre at Provincial House in Wellington Parade, East Melbourne. Melbourne's Catholic newspaper, *The Advocate*, reported that there were to be two Natural Family Planning Centres in the city.

From 1971 onwards, Dr Santamaria, who by then was head of St Vincent's Hospital Department of Community Medicine, provided the opportunity for a weekly Billings evening clinic at the hospital. Dr Santamaria had graduated from St Vincent's hospital in 1948.

> At that stage I addressed John Billings as Sir, a member of a new breed of exciting staff members who had been trained overseas and were anxious to develop the new specialised departments in medicine and surgery. As a student, I was interested in medico-moral matters and I soon realised that Dr John Billings was a pre-eminent figure in the field of medicine and his image became more and more that of an articulate Catholic physician at the forefront of medicine in Australia.

Dr Santamaria, who went on to become a physician, oncologist and haematologist and public health specialist, had been aware of John Billings' involvement in natural family planning since about 1955. Their friendship was forged, however, in the heat of battle in 1967 when the medical profession was coming to terms with the Abortion Act in the UK, which legalised abortions for the first time by registered practitioners and Melbourne GP Dr Bertram Wainer launched a campaign for law reform in Australia. Dr Santamaria recalls that he, John Billings, Dr Frank Hayden and Dr Eric Seal "formed the Victorian branch of the Human Life Research Foundation which was the forerunner of the Right to Life movement in Australia."

For those intent on promoting natural methods of birth control the split between the Drs Billings and their team on the one hand and advocates of the Sympto-Thermal Method on the other was highly unfortunate, causing confusion and anxiety among prospective users as well as health professionals. It weakened the impact of natural family planning in the wider marketplace, at a time when lifestyles were becoming freer and artificial contraception more readily available. Women seeking assistance with natural family planning found the advice they were given varied depending on what state of Australia they lived in, or which diocese or organisation controlled the clinic they visited. It's little wonder that many couples, including those in "mixed" marriages where one partner was Catholic and the other not, gave up in confusion and sought a prescription for the Pill from the doctor, which in many cases proved unsatisfactory in terms of side-effects.

Another split in the natural family planning ranks opened

up several decades later between John and Evelyn Billings and US medical consultant in obstetrics, gynaecology and reproductive medicine Dr Thomas Hilgers MD. The Billings had much in common with Dr Hilgers, the director of the Pope Paul VI Institute in Omaha, Nebraska, who together with his co-workers developed the Creighton Model FertilityCare System and in 2004 published *The Medical and Surgical Practice of NaProTECHNOLOGY*.

Dr Hilgers, who was appointed as a permanent member of the Pontifical Academy for Life in 1994, was a strong admirer of the Billings Method, describing the Ovulation Method as "one of the most important discoveries of the 20th century". John Billings' account of a medical conference in Madras, India, in January 1983 records that Dr Hilgers "gave an excellent paper on his research and also showed an ultrasound movie which demonstrates the early development of the child in the uterus." According to the account, Dr Hilgers compared discovery of the Ovulation method "with the discovery of Penicillin" and "expressed the view that the full potential of the Ovulation method has yet to be achieved."

The Billings were deeply unhappy, however, over the promotion of the Creighton Model and NaProTECHNOLOGY (natural procreative technology) as "A Standardized Modification of the Billings system". Dr Hilgers' systems have built up a strong following, including in Australia. In a strongly worded paper issued in 2006, that delved into medical details that would be beyond the scope of most lay readers, John and Evelyn

Billings insisted:

> "The methods are fundamentally different and should be kept separate. We object emphatically to the changes made to the BOM by Dr Hilgers in his textbook. They reveal a deep non-understanding of the Billings Ovulation Method. There was no consultation with us to modify or standardise the "Billings Method". The result has been destructive and confusing to many couples. The BOM remains as described in the authentic WOOMB (World Organisation of the Ovulation Method Billings) literature – not as modified by Dr Hilgers.'[2]

Contacted for a response for this book, Dr Hilgers replied:

> While they did write a strongly worded paper issued in the year 2006, that paper, while it was referred to as an assessment of "NaProTECHNOLOGY," dealt with only the first 200 pages of our medical textbook (which is 1,244 pages long).
>
> These first pages deal with the CREIGHTON MODEL Fertility*Care*™System and do not deal specifically with the application of NaProTECHNOLOGY. I did not change the Billings Ovulation Method, nor did I refer to it in any fashion as the Billings Ovulation Method. In research circles, there was no need to seek consultation because we were no longer working with the "Billings Method." I cannot comment on what is referred to as "destructive and confusing to many couples" because, in the world of the CREIGHTON MODEL System, this actually has led to a much better understanding of the phases of fertility and infertility because of a standardized language which has been developed and is objective and no longer subjective. I totally agree, incidentally, that, "The Billings Ovulation

Method remains as described in the authentic WOOMB literature – not as modified by Dr. Hilgers." Never in my imagination would I think that the use of the terminology, *"A standardized modification of the Billings System"* would create so much difficulty for them. I had absolutely no intention of that. I was just trying to give them the proper credit for their work that led to what I believe is one of the most extraordinary compliments to their work that has ever been accomplished.

Dr Hilgers also said he will "try very hard" never to use the terminology, "a standardized modification of the Billings Ovulation Method", again. ''While, frankly, I hate to do this because I think it undermines the very contribution of Drs John and Lyn Billings, I feel that I need to because it has apparently caused them great despair; and I have no interest in being a part of that."

Regardless of the disagreement over terminology, Dr Hilgers has consistently been magnanimous and fulsome in his praise of the Drs Billings, telling Bishop Anthony Fisher, who is also a member of the Pontifical Academy for Life, that "it was a scandal that the medical profession, the medical academy and places such as the Nobel Foundation had not honoured them more." He has often said publicly that "as a gynaecologist, I probably would never have discovered this system. It took a neurologist and a paediatrician, doctors who are trained to listen to define the basic concepts. And for those skills that the Drs. Billings possessed, I am deeply, deeply appreciative."

Dr Hilgers believes:

With regard to the "split" between the Drs. Billings and their team on the one hand and advocates of the Sympto-Thermal Method on the other, I personally think that far too much is made of these things. There are very significant differences between the different natural methods and it is not possible to have expertise in all methods (although I have studied them all and have published on them, I do not consider myself an overall expert on all of the different methodologies).

When people in authority or of influence are weak in their calling to do something about natural family planning, they often refer to the "split" between the different methodologies without knowing much at all about the methodologies. Thus, what the Drs. Billings developed was quite different than other methodologies, and while at times their words were occasionally (and rarely) intemperate, that could be said for all of us. The most important thing is that all methodologies be taught well and to the highest level of quality capable within those systems. This is something that I have said publicly on many different occasions.

Dr Hilgers' involvement with natural family planning began in December 1968 when he was a 4th year medical student at the University of Minnesota and has been uninterrupted over the past 44 years. He remains warm in his praise of John and Evelyn Billings. For him:

> Hearing Dr John Billings speak in June 1972 on the Ovulation Method opened up, for me, a whole new way of thinking when it came to a natural method of family planning. Keep in mind that I am a gynaecologist, not a neurologist or a paediatrician. Much of what we have

accomplished with what now has become known as the CREIGHTON MODEL Fertility*Care*™System is the result of the standardisation of the mucus observations that we were able to accomplish early in our research years between 1976 and 1978. The 'we' that I refer to are my wife, Susan K. Hilgers, and 2 nurses from St. Louis, K. Diane Daly, RN, and Ann M. Prebil, RN."

In the United States, the growth and development of NaProTECHNOLOGY is increasing at a rapid rate and Dr Hilgers has found the system has allowed many Catholic doctors to come back to their faith:

We have trained over 2,370 teachers of the CREIGHTON MODEL System of which about 500 of them are medical doctors. We have a full one-year Fellowship in Medical & Surgical NaProTECHNOLOGY for postgraduate obstetrician-gynaecologists. These are individuals who are able to use surgical NaProTECHNOLOGY protocols in a way which is extremely helpful to women's health. NaProTECHNOLOGY looks at the underlying root causes of problems and tries to solve them.

Even some of the Billings' strongest supporters in Melbourne recognised that John Billings, in particular, could be stubborn and pugnacious in occasionally shunning individuals with whom he disagreed on small or even moot points. One of Dr Hilgers' deepest regrets is that "over many decades of having the opportunity to meet with, eat with and discuss the work of the Drs Billings with them, they pretty much ignored discussing with me any of the work that we were doing. I truly believe that they have not had a good understanding of what we have accomplished."

If progress is to be made with Natural Family Planning in the west, Dr Hilgers has a point when he says "There is no need for either rivalry or antagonism, but rather honour and respect that should be shown to each other." Melbourne's John Paul II Institute for Marriage and the Family, established by George Pell when he was Archbishop of Melbourne, is one teaching institution that has taken a broad, positive approach, introducing three methods of Natural Family Planning to the students – the Sympto-Thermal, Billings Ovulation and Creighton Model methods to enable their students to work effectively in areas using any of the methods.

For all its strengths, the BOM needs a booster if it is to re-establish a similar footing in Australia to what the Creighton Model and NaProTECHNOLOGY are enjoying across the Pacific. Some patients who have used the Creighton Model were reassured by the fact that it was taught by a doctor. On the other hand, one of the strengths of the Billings Method has been the fact that it has been widely disseminated by non-medical instructors, which is useful in poorer countries where doctors and nurses are scarce.

Aside from the confusion created by rival NFP methods in Australia over the years, another long-standing problem has been that some of those promoting such methods within the Church and elsewhere have been poor advocates. At the best of times the subject is sensitive and unsuitable for Sunday sermons, which are the main contacts between priests and most of their people.

In the 1970s and 1980s, on special parish missions which afforded the time and opportunity for such matters to be raised, priests keen to increase awareness of natural family planning also tended to speak about breast feeding, elaborated on their view that "a mother's place was in the home", articulated their support for the fiscally irresponsible concept of a "homemakers allowance" and criticised the so-called "contraceptive mentality" which some clerics claimed they could detect "even if people were not actually using contraception."

However well-intentioned and sincere, such a mix of messages often backfired, especially among the key target group of young women finding their feet in an era when they were being encouraged at school to broaden their horizons and grasp the opportunities offered by education and careers. Such priests and others were, of course, entitled to their opinions and some, in retrospect, held merit. But popular as this worldview was in some quarters, the approach was destined to fail at a time when attitudes were changing.

Being told that "even illiterate women in third world countries" could use the Method, a point reiterated by well-meaning missionary priests who did not have a clue about young women's aspirations, did nothing to enhance the appeal of natural family planning to urban sophisticates in Australia. Some women revisited the subject later of their own accord, however, prompted by the unexpected all-day nausea and non-existent libido they found after trying the pill. In hindsight, a smarter strategy might have been to promote natural family planning by urging young women not to "sell yourself short" or "accept second best" in terms of chemicals and devices and to insist that their male partners shoulder their fair share of responsibility for family planning.

This was how Dr Evelyn Billings saw the issue. In her view, the Billings Method was the best and safest form of family planning because it is reliable and because it is natural. From the outset, the organisation promoting the method operated independently from the Church and other organisations. At the same time, had the process of information and dissemination been better supported and handled by Church authorities who theoretically had a strong interest in its success, long-term usage of the Billings Method might have been much greater in Australia, especially as secular family planning providers acknowledge that it is highly reliable when used correctly. Such issues, however, were and are rarely raised in Catholic schools, prompting Archbishop Pell to remark, when he was in charge of the Archdiocese of Melbourne, that "it's easier to have the Billings Method taught in Communist China than in Catholic schools." And as late as 2012, prospective patients seeking information in some Australian capital cities were briefed on the Sympto-Thermal Method, involving the inconvenience of daily temperature monitoring.

As medical professionals, the Billings were determined that their method would be backed with detailed scientific research. In addition to Professor Brown's affirmation, the accuracy of their guidelines for avoiding and achieving pregnancy were also established in the 1970s by Professor Erik Odeblad of Umea, Sweden, a physicist and obstetrician/gynaecologist who spent much of his professional life studying the complexity of the female cervix.

The Billings also began a long collaboration with Sydney GP Dr Kevin Hume, who introduced the Method to Sydney and further afield and later ensured it had a presence at UN women's conferences. Early and subsequent trials of the Billings method found it was 97-99 per cent effective in avoiding pregnancy if used correctly and 75 per cent effective for helping previously infertile couples trying to conceive.

By the time John Billings was made a Knight Commander of the Order of St Gregory the Great (KCSG) by Pope Paul VI in 1969 for "Service to the Family" the "longest three months in history" had stretched to 14 years. And that was just the beginning.

---

1. "The Life and Times of John J. Billings: The Mucus Symptom, a Physiologic Marker of Women's Fertility", by Charles W. Norris. *Linacre Quarterly*, Catholic Medical Association. August 2010. http://lq.cathmed.metapress.com/content/f9n2120730221m85/

2. http://www.woomb.org/omrrca/BOMvCrMS.pdf

Dr Evelyn Billings, 1970s

Drs John and Lyn Billings with Pope Paul VI

4
The Times They were a Changin'

Across the world, 1968 was a year of rebellion and upheaval as the anti-Vietnam war movement – closely linked to wider student protests against almost every form of established authority – gathered momentum. So did militant feminism, sexual liberation, the counter-culture and the importance of the post-war Baby Boomers, the rising generation whom 12 months earlier had been declared collectively *Time* Magazine's "Man of the Year" (since amended to "Person of the Year").

It was also the year when Martin Luther King and Robert Kennedy were assassinated and the year the Prague Spring blossomed, only to be crushed by Soviet tanks. Its ideals were destined to wait another 30 years to reach fruition. In a world eager for modernism and social change, 25 July 1968 saw the issuing of what was surely the most controversial encyclical in papal history, Pope Paul VI's *Humanae Vitae*. Contrary to the advice of the Vatican's own Pontifical Commission on Birth Control comprised of clerics and laity from five continents, the encyclical barred Catholics from using what many regarded as one of the most liberating developments in history – reliable artificial birth control, especially the Pill.

Fast forward almost half a century and it is virtually impossible for today's younger and middle-aged Catholics to comprehend the angst surrounding *Humanae Vitae* in their parents' and grandparents' generation. Some loved the encyclical, many hated it and some worried that it would inevitably be ignored by the vast majority of the laity, introducing widespread disobedience to a serious Church teaching as never before in Catholic life. That indeed proved to be the case, with Catholics, supported by more liberal priests, nuns and teachers increasingly relying on "individual conscience" to disregard traditional teaching on Sunday Mass going and in some cases, even abortion.

At the time it appeared, *Humanae Vitae* provoked a cutting-edge moral theology debate inside and outside the church, which is not easy to comprehend in light of many more difficult issues on today's agenda including embryonic screening and experimentation, embryonic stem cell treatments, IVF, abortion, same-sex marriage and the clerical abuse scandals that have eroded so much of the Church's moral authority.

Two months after the encyclical was published, the Canadian bishops issued their controversial Winnipeg Statement, in which they urged the faithful to "examine in all honesty their reaction to what he (Pope Paul VI) has said." A certain number of Catholics, they argued "although admittedly subject to the teaching of the encyclical, find it either extremely difficult or even impossible to make their own all elements of this doctrine ...

"In accord with the accepted principles of moral theology, if these persons have tried sincerely but without success to pursue a line of conduct in keeping with the given directives, they may be safely assured that whoever honestly chooses that course which seems right to him does so in good conscience."

Confessors were told to "show sympathetic understanding and reverence for the sincere good faith of those who fail in their effort to accept some point of the encyclical."[1]

In a follow-up statement a year later, the bishops toned down the Winnipeg statement, adding:

> We wish to reiterate our positive conviction that a Catholic Christian is not free to form his conscience without consideration of the teaching of the *magisterium*, in the particular instance exercised by the Holy Father in an encyclical letter. It is false and dangerous to maintain that because this encyclical has not demanded "the absolute assent of faith", any Catholic may put it aside as if it had never appeared. On the contrary, such teaching in some ways imposes a great burden of responsibility on the individual conscience.

Forty years later, in a sharper reversal of their predecessors' original, liberal position, the Canadian Bishops' Conference issued a pastoral letter entitled "Liberating Potential", inviting Catholics "to discover or rediscover," the message of *Humanae Vitae*.

The bishops wrote:

> How can we fail to recognise its prophetic character when we consider the troubling evolution of two fundamental human institutions, marriage and the family? Both continue to be affected by the contraceptive mentality feared and rejected in the encyclical of Pope Paul VI. And what can be said of the future demographic deficit confronting Western societies? This is not to imply that there is no legitimate concern for natural family planning and spacing births in a couple's experience.

Nevertheless, *Humanae Vitae* is much more than a "no to contraception". This encyclical is in reality a major reflection on God's design for human love. It proposes a vision of "the whole man and the whole mission to which he is called ... both its natural, earthly aspects, and its supernatural, eternal aspects. It is an invitation to be open to the grandeur, beauty and dignity of the Creator's call to the vocation of marriage.²

Credit for the fact that the Billings Ovulation Method has been widely accepted in Canada rests with Father Joseph Hattie OMI, an oblate priest who first encountered the Method in the early 1970s while working as a priest/teacher in a secondary school in Ontario. Father Hattie also promoted the method when he was Catholic Chaplain at Dalhousie University in Halifax, Nova Scotia, in the late 1970s.

L-R Fr Joseph Hattie OMI, Drs John and Lyn Billings

As he recalled in a speech in Melbourne in 2001: "I was originally impressed with its simplicity, especially compared with the *Sympto-Thermal Method* I was familiar with." He was to become one of John and Lyn's closest friends and a keen source of spiritual support and remained in contact with Lyn by telephone for years.

In an interview for this book, Australia's leading bioethicist, Bishop Anthony Fisher of Parramatta, who is a Dominican friar, a member of the Pontifical Academy for Life and Professor of Moral Theology and Bioethics in the John Paul II Institute for Marriage and the Family in Melbourne, acknowledged the dichotomies of the present situation in which the Church says little about its opposition to contraception, nevertheless maintaining that teaching "on the books" while it is quietly ignored by many of the faithful.

> Developments in the last 50 years have rather overshadowed the issue of contraception. Partly due to the contraceptive mentality or culture that evolved, and for other reasons, we've had a sexual revolution, a copulation explosion rather than a population explosion, unthinkable rates of abortion, the creation and destruction of millions of human embryos in the lab, you name it. So contraception, which is clearly a less grave matter than some of these, naturally got less attention as the Church fought a rear-guard action on some of these issues.

Bishop Fisher also admitted that "bishops and priests have been remiss in not preaching more on this subject – perhaps for fear of upsetting many of their people." The relative silence, he said, "might have left John and Lyn feeling rather lonely at times, even abandoned by the Church they were trying to serve." Lyn said she wished priests and bishops would raise the matter more often, but realised it was not the best topic for sermons at Sunday Masses.

The Church's teaching on artificial contraception remains clear, however. As Bishop Fisher summed it up:

> Any action which in advance, during or after intercourse aims to render procreation impossible, as a means or an end is held by the Church to be intrinsically wrong (see *Catechism of the Catholic Church* 2370, citing *Humanae Vitae* 14). Pope John Paul II couched the issue in terms of the innate, conjugal "language of the body" rather than the natural law discourse that Paul VI used, but both were in clear agreement on this. Contraception, on John Paul's account, is a "contradictory language" to the language of "total reciprocal self-giving of husband and wife" (see *Catechism* 2370 citing *Familiaris Consortio* 32). Recently, Pope Benedict XVI linked the issue with *respect for life* and *development* issues (in *Caritas in Veritate* 28). The issue has therefore been repeatedly raised in exercises of the papal magisterium in the last fifty years or so with the Church's teaching remaining unchanged. That same teaching asked medical researchers to find positive ways forward for people and John and Evelyn Billings are the most outstanding respondents to that call from the Popes.

Bishop Fisher finds clerical reticence to discuss contraception "strange really: we're not afraid of preaching against speeding, lying or adultery, even though many people do these as well." Another reason for the diffidence about talking about contraception, he said "might be the sexual abuse scandals that have affected the credibility of the Church as a teacher about sexuality in many people's minds and perhaps undermined the confidence of pastors to talk about such subjects. It never stopped John Paul II who addressed the matter openly and confidently and repeatedly throughout the 80s and 90s."

One of the most serious reasons advanced by Bishop Fisher for Catholics and others to embrace natural family planning is the early abortifacient effect of the most popular contraceptives. Bishop Fisher said:

> The IUD has an abortifacient effect because it prevents the fertilised egg from implanting in the wall of the womb. Likewise, the 'contraceptive pill' cannot be understood solely as a contraceptive because it is likely that decreased estrogen content in the 'low dose pill' will have an increased endometrial effect, which causes the loss of the zygote if there has been a conception.
>
> Any drug or device that has an abortifacient effect is to be condemned because, by destroying an embryo, it causes an abortion of a newly conceived human person; but most women using the Pill or IUD are probably unaware of this risk and so not morally culpable. Drugs and devices that risk killing an early human being are of serious moral concern for Catholics and others.

In terms of the basic biological facts about the operation of contraceptives, Bishop Fisher's argument is supported by a writer from a different perspective. In her book *The Whole Woman* in 1999 feminist Germaine Greer wrote:

> These days, contraception is abortion, because the third-generation Pills cannot be shown to prevent sperm

fertilising an ovum. Yet no one feels so strongly against abortion at any stage that they picket the factories where birth control pills are produced.

IUDs are clearly abortifacient: these devices work by creating inflammation of the uterus, often accompanied by infection. Women who accept them as contraceptive devices are actually being equipped with a do-it-yourself abortionist's tool. The outcome is frequent occult abortion, heavy bleeding and pelvic inflammatory disease, with the accompanying elevated risk of ectopic pregnancy.

Whether you feel that the creation and wastage of so many embryos is an important issue or not, you must see that the cynical deception of millions of women by selling abortifacients as if they were contraceptives is incompatible with the respect due to women as human beings.

You must also see that expecting women to be grateful for the opportunity to have inserted into their bodies instruments for sucking and scraping out the products of avoidable conception shows them as much contempt.

Fake contraceptive technology manipulates women in ways that we are coming to condemn when they are practised on members of other species. What women don't know does hurt them.

If we ask ourselves whether we would have any hope of imposing upon men the duty to protect women's fertility and their health, and avoid the abortions that occur in their uncounted millions every day, we will see in a blinding light how unfree women are. Women, from the youngest to the oldest, are aware that to impose conditions on intimacy would be to be accorded even less of it than they get already.[3]

Ethicist Nicholas Tonti-Filippini also explored the issue in the *Linacre Quarterly* journal of medical ethics in February 1995, noting

> ...a gradual but major change in oral contraception. The drive to reduce metabolic assault and unwanted side-effects has resulted in a trend toward formulations which are less contraceptive and more likely to be abortifacient. This has a broad range of moral consequences.
>
> The estrogen content is significant in suppressing ovulation. The lower the estrogen dose, the greater the likelihood that ovulation will not be suppressed. In the latter case, the cervical and endometrial factors are more significant. In the various formulations, it is not known how often ovulation is not suppressed and the cervical factor fails to block the passage of sperm and so allows fertilisation followed by an endometrial effect causing loss of the zygote. However it is likely that that is sometimes the result of taking oral contraception and it is more likely in the circumstances of the newer formulations with their much lower estrogen content and reduced effect on ovulation. The likely induced loss rate of zygotes, though low, is of serious moral significance because it is human life at risk.
>
> The progesterone-only formulations are more likely to have this unfortunate abortifacient result than the combined estrogen-progestogen formulations.
>
> The 'contraceptive pill' (meaning either the combined estrogen and progestogen preparations or the progestogen only preparations) ought not be regarded as contraceptive only. There is a significant chance of abortifacient effect which increases as the estrogen content diminishes.

> The increased likelihood of the various formulations being abortifacient changes the moral evaluation of material cooperation by health professionals in regard to contraception. The grave matter of justice and respect for nascent human life arises.
>
> There is a need for clear teaching on contraceptive-abortifacients and the deceit involved, not only in order to address the matter of respect for human life, but also the matter of the rights of women to know what they are doing to their own bodies and to the lives for whom their bodies are rendered hostile. Such a statement might also address the moral conclusions that flow from that information in regard to the practice of contraception and abortifacience and the issue of cooperation.
>
> Also to be considered are the new birth control developments other than the estrogen-progestogen pill. The new preparations are nearly all abortifacient, although they are usually trialled, approved and/or marketed misleadingly as 'contraceptive'.[5]

Dissent and confusion were rife after the release of *Humanae Vitae* in 1968. Many priests and religious did not bother to hide their dismay and many families struggled to live with the Papal teaching, with some staying away from Holy Communion if they felt unable to live up to its demands. At the same time, many women suffered side-effects from the Pill and quietly worried about its long term implications.

Against this background, Lyn and John Billings believed they had an important message to promote – a highly reliable but natural way of preventing conception. It was far superior to the hit-and-miss practice of guessing what was the "safe period" for making love without conceiving, and less cumbersome than the Symptom-Thermal Method. John's brother Bob Billings, who shared a similar outlook, did his part, as did many other Catholic pharmacists of the era, in refusing to stock artificial contraception. Some Catholic doctors also refused to prescribe the Pill for contraceptive use.

It was a confusing and anxious time for many lay Catholics. In the wider world, the tide had been turning in favour of contraception since the 1920s, when an intense debate within the Anglican Communion resulted in the 1930 Lambeth Conference resolving that "Where there is a clearly felt moral obligation to limit or avoid parenthood, complete abstinence is the primary and obvious method." At the same time, the Conference decided if a morally sound reason existed for avoiding abstinence "the Conference agrees that other methods may be used, provided that this is done in the light of Christian principles."[5]

By 1958, when contraception was a way of life for most Anglicans, the Lambeth Conference went further, resolving that the responsibility for deciding upon the number and frequency of children was laid by God upon the consciences of parents "in such ways as are acceptable to husband and wife".

The issue also attracted attention within Catholic ranks in the first half of the 20th century, with Pope Pius XI issuing his encyclical *Casti Connubi* on 31 December 1930 in response to the Lambeth resolution of that year. It reaffirmed Catholic opposition to artificial birth control.[6]

The medical approval and release of the contraceptive Pill in the early 1960s, however, brought calls for a rethink, with some theologians and Catholic doctors initially arguing that the pill, unlike barrier methods of contraception, was acceptable for Catholic use. Dr Santamaria recalls: "A great controversy evolved among Catholic theologians about the moral licitness of the use of the pill, at a time when natural methods of fertility control were perceived as somewhat primitive and of limited effectiveness."

Pope John XXIII established a commission of six theologians to study the issue in 1963, and this was later expanded by Paul VI to include 15 Cardinals and bishops and 64 lay people. After two years' study of the issues, the lay people reportedly voted 60 to 4 and the bishops 9 to 6 to liberalise the church's position and permit the use of the pill.

Dr Santamaria remembers that "many priests in the confessional were telling people that the matter was still subjudice and they should follow their own consciences until the question was resolved." Many did, and became accustomed to the Pill, especially after the majority report supporting a change in Catholic teaching was leaked to the press in the United States in 1967, adding to the widespread expectation that change was imminent. Dr Santamaria and the Drs Billings, however, after studying the history of Church teaching on the issue, were always confident that this would not be the case. They were correct. Paul VI discounted the advice of his commission and adopted the view of the minority of bishops, including Polish archbishop, Karol Wojtyla, who argued against any change, partly on the grounds that it would violate the natural moral law by separating the unitive and procreative aspects of sexuality.

Another concern raised in the minority report was that: "If it should be declared that contraception is not evil in itself, then we should have to concede frankly that the Holy Spirit had been on the side of the Protestant churches in 1930 (when the encyclical *Casti Connubi* was promulgated)."[7]

Many others expressed the opposite point of view, including Professor Hans Küng, then a leading Catholic theologian:

> This teaching [against contraceptive birth control] has laid a heavy burden on the conscience of innumerable people, even in industrially developed countries with declining birth rates. But for the people in many under-developed countries, especially in Latin America, it constitutes a source of incalculable harm, a crime in which the Church has implicated itself.[8]

Evelyn Billings supported *Humanae Vitae* among other reasons because she believed that the Ovulation Method was safer and more reliable than any contraceptive. She remembers that the encyclical "brought a lot of people into the Centre – they came in droves from that point on. And we were ready."

While the encyclical surprised many it inspired rather than surprised Lyn and her husband. John wrote about it in 2004, recalling Paul VI's encouragement to "men of science" who "can considerably advance the welfare of marriage and the family, along with peace of conscience, if by pooling their efforts they labour to explain more thoroughly the various conditions favouring the proper regulation of births." John also recalled "the wish already expressed by Pope Pius XII, that medical science succeed in providing a sufficiently secure basis for a regulation of births, founded on the observance of natural rhythms."

While a hard teaching, *Humanae Vitae* was prescient in so far as it recognised that the widespread use of contraception would "open wide the way for marital infidelity and a general lowering of moral standards." Paul VI feared that "a man who grows accustomed to the use of contraceptive methods may forget the reverence due to a woman, and, disregarding her physical and emotional equilibrium, reduce her to being a mere instrument for the satisfaction of his own desires, no longer considering her as his partner whom he should surround with care and affection." Millions of women from different cultures would attest to the veracity of that insight.

In an article to mark the 30th anniversary of *Humanae Vitae* in 1998 the then-Catholic Archbishop of Melbourne, George Pell, posed the question: "Are families better off today? Are more young people happy? The debate over the Pill is a point of entry to the bigger questions of sexuality, marriage and the family. For our well-being, perhaps even our survival, these too must be considered." Whereas contraception could make couples "selfish in the demands they make of each other," NFP fostered "a deeper attentiveness and tenderness towards one's spouse."[9]

In hindsight, even some of the Church's most loyal sons believe the issue could have been better handled, though it is doubtful if the public reaction would have been substantially different in the Western world in the midst of so many upheavals. US intellectual George Weigel, in his definitive biography of Pope John Paul II, *Witness to Hope,* argues that while the encyclical was always going to be controversial "it might not have been so debilitating had the Pope taken Cardinal Wojtyla's counsel more thoroughly."

As Weigel noted, the Archbishop of Krakow had created his own diocesan commission to study the issues being debated by the Papal Commission. While it arrived at the same conclusion as Pope Paul VI its approach, Weigel argues, was more effective. The Krakow commission looked beyond both "stupid conservatism" or a deconstruction of the moral theology to develop "a new framework for the Church's classic position on conjugal morality and fertility regulation: a fully articulated, philosophically well-developed Christian humanism that believers and non-believers alike could engage."[10]

In arguments better fitted to the dignity of the human person, especially women, that Pope John Paul II later used in his Theology of the Body in the 1980s, the Krakow commission said: "The number of children called into existence cannot be left to chance" but needed to be decided "in a dialogue of love between husband and wife." Family planning, it concluded, should recognise "cooperation" of the spouses. The Pill and the IUD, to the contrary, freed men from responsibility while women carried the risks with methods that were intrusive and potentially harmful.

Following the release of the encyclical, doctors including Joe Santamaria noticed that many of their Catholic colleagues studiously avoided openly supporting Church teaching. Most clergy, too, ceased preaching on birth control. While the vast majority of clergy and laity remained silent, the topic remained hotly contested between the Church's most outspoken liberal theologians on the one hand and those who actively backed natural family planning on the other and who came to be identified as "conservatives" and "traditionalists".

Pope John Paul II's Theology of the Body and encyclical *Evangelium Vitae* reignited the issue briefly during the 1980s, arousing the interest of a new generation of young Catholics who have been influenced by their experiences at World Youth Days. For most Catholics, however, the question became a non-issue, opening up a vast gap between official Church teaching and the everyday lives of Catholics. As the impact of *Humanae Vitae* waned, even friends and some family members believed that John and Evelyn Billings were "flogging a dead horse"

Papal Audience, front row from L, Kath Smyth, Dr Kevin Hume, Dr (Sr) Anna Cappella, Dr Evelyn Billings, Dr John Billings, Pope John Paul II

with the Ovulation Method. Their passion for spreading news of the Method, however, took on a missionary zeal and produced surprising outcomes.

1. http://www.u.arizona.edu/~aversa/modernism/winnipeg.html
2. http://www.cccb.ca/site/images/stories/pdf/humanae_vitae_en.pdf
3. *The Whole Woman* by Germaine Greer, Doubleday. 1999
4. "The Pill: Abortifacient or Contraceptive? A Literature Review" by Nicholas Tonti-Filippini, BA, MA, Linacre Quarterly, February 1995, pp. 5-10
5. http://www.churchofengland.org/our-views/medical-ethics-health-social-care-policy/contraception.aspx
6. http://www.vatican.va/holy_father/pius_xi/encyclicals/documents/hf_p-xi_enc_31121930_casti-connubii_en.html
7. http://churchandstate.org.uk/2010/06/why-the-church-cant-change/
8. http://www.population-security.org/swom-98-02.htm
9. http://www.ad2000.com.au/articles/1998/sep1998p3_546.html
10. *Witness to Hope* by George Weigel. Harper Collins. 1999

John and Lyn in Africa with Dr Kevin Hume in background

5
Building Momentum

By 1980, the Ovulation Method, as John and Evelyn initially called their system, had been officially renamed the Billings Ovulation Method (BOM) at the suggestion of the World Health Organisation to differentiate it from other systems of natural family planning. Within Australia, it was largely disseminated person by person, group by group by word of mouth, especially among women. Internationally, the message was spread in a more organised way, through organisations affiliated with the Church and through the medical profession.

Like other women of their generation, Marian Corkill and WOOMB's archivist Merilyn Kennealy first encountered the Billings in the early 1970s. As young, married Catholic mothers, the doctors' message resonated. Marian first heard Lyn speak at her local Parish hall, while Merilyn hosted her at a function for like-minded women at home in the same parish, St Martin of Tours, Rosanna, in Melbourne's north east. It was from that same parish that several other women, who became senior Billings teachers and organisers were drawn, including Kath Smyth and Marie Marshall. Lyn's audiences found her gentle and approachable, a mother who shared their interests.

A decade later, in 1981, another young couple who were inspired by a talk given by Lyn and John were Stephen and Joan

Clements. Father Catarinich, their parish priest, had already introduced them to the Ovulation Method and they had made up their minds to follow it. Listening to the Billings, however, was a "life changing" experience for Joan, who became involved in promoting it as a volunteer teacher and later as a Director of WOOMB (World Organisation of the Ovulation Method Billings) International Ltd and member of the Education Committee. Joan, who is manager of the Vocations Office for the Catholic Archdiocese of Melbourne, has trained teachers of the Billings Ovulation Method in China, Singapore and New Zealand and more recently, has completed six trips to Vietnam over three years to introduce the Method there. In 2010 Joan addressed a study seminar of the Pontifical Council for the Family in Rome on how the Method is helping to promote the Culture of Life in Oceania. "It has really become an apostolate for Stephen and me, an apostolate which has afforded me fantastic opportunities. I could never have imagined myself doing any of these things if I had not heard John and Lyn speak on that day back in 1981."

While far removed, in most ways, from the feminist ideology espoused in *The Female Eunuch* published in 1970, Lyn's message was also one of female empowerment. Women, she argued have the right to understand their own fertility and the right to avoid conception through scientifically-proven means that avoid side-effects. She and John also recognised early on that the best teachers of their method would be women themselves – not doctors, nurses and paramedics – but well-instructed women with empathy and good communication skills. From the outset, the Billings Ovulation Method was taught primarily by a network of female instructors, in their own homes and more recently in professional settings such as medical centres. Teaching materials were developed and teacher training began in Melbourne in the early 1970s, initially at St Vincent's and at Provincial House. Hundreds of teachers in all Australian states, from Cairns to Perth, have subsequently been trained by the Billings organisation. Their contact details are available from the head office in Melbourne, and the website www.thebillingsovulationmethod.org

Beyond the fact that their method fitted with the Church's approval of natural family planning, Drs John and Evelyn believed that it was more reliable than barrier methods of contraception such as condoms and the diaphragm and medically superior to the IUD and the pill, both of which carried side-effects. John Billings also envisaged the wider benefits the method could provide, predicting, with some prescience: "One of these days I believe it will be recognised as a diagnostic resource."

In a few cases, women well-schooled in the method have been able to notice abnormal mucus patterns that on medical investigation proved to be early signs of serious illnesses such as Polycystic Ovarian Syndrome (PCOS) and cervical cancer. John Billings wrote in relation to one patient in 2004: "It is not too much to say that knowing the BOM probably saved her life because it led to appropriate treatment of the cancer at the earliest possible moment."

Despite the obstacles in the wider society and within the natural family planning sphere, John and Evelyn Billings worked hard to ensure that news of their Method travelled around the world, prompting invitations for them to travel far and wide. Their first trip, in 1968, was a teaching trip to New Zealand. The following year they visited Malaysia and Hong Kong and in 1970 they visited five central American countries, with Evelyn also travelling to Panama for a discussion with the local Archbishop and John to Washington DC to talk about the Method to the International Institute of Health.

Arrival at yet another international airport

These trips were the beginnings of what was to be millions of miles of air travel on more than 100 international conference and teaching visits to five continents over the next 25 years. Most of the trips were strenuous and demanding, often extending for at least three weeks and taking in several countries. In August 1979, for example, John and Lyn visited Lesotho, Kenya and Rwanda, where they encountered hunger, privation, tribal culture and a mix of vibrant Catholic faith and superstition.

John Billings wrote detailed accounts of many of these trips, which are filed in the WOOMB archives in Melbourne. The accounts, many of them running to 30 single-typed pages of impeccable prose, were an aide memoir and he did not intend details of meetings with individuals and organisations to be published. The general tone of the writing and the detail of the accounts reveal that he and Lyn were passionate advocates for their Method and had a strong empathy with people from many walks of life and cultures.

In the Philippines in 1988, where Mother Teresa invited them to instruct her Missionaries of Charity in how to teach the Method, they encountered appalling poverty "just as bad as anything we have previously observed in Calcutta, Bombay or Madras or in Latin America." They were especially moved by the children they encountered who were suffering through the entirely preventable problems of malnutrition and tuberculosis. While the Billings recognised that their Method would be of enormous help to poverty-stricken families who were struggling to feed the children they already had, they were implacably opposed to the notion of surgical sterilisation, even under such fraught circumstances. Many would disagree vehemently, but John wrote in Manila: "It is a gross cruelty to destroy the fertility of people who have no material possessions."

Injustice made them deeply uncomfortable. Arriving in South Africa in 1979 John observed that "the beautiful food and wines reinforced the message that South Africa is the country that has everything – everything, that is, except justice, a fact of which I had been immediately reminded when the black housemaid at the hotel called me "Master". However, even South Africa is not without hope."

Later that trip he and Evelyn conducted workshops in Kenya, where they found rural women working with little rest from the time they rose at 5.30 am to gather firewood and carry water. "If the baby should cry she is recalled by her husband to attend to the baby," John wrote. After preparing breakfast the woman "rouses her husband" after which she cleans up the house before both head to the cornfields to work. "It is regarded as being beneath the man's dignity to appear in the kitchen at any time." At night, in the worst circumstances, women were beaten if they fell asleep before their husbands.

In the Billings' view, their Ovulation Method offered the promise of a transformative effect as it required both partners to take responsibility for family planning and for the husband to understand his wife's natural cycle. Describing such a case he encountered in Kenya John wrote:

> The husband of one of the couples undergoing the teacher-training course told us that for many years he had behaved

'like an animal' towards his wife. He beat her frequently and had no concern for her at all.

Then, more than a year ago, they had been given instruction together in the Ovulation Method and their relationship had undergone a remarkable change; he now felt strongly drawn to his wife in a new understanding of her and had come to love her deeply. This particular individual, a tall, strong and well-educated African said that with the O.M. 'something wonderful is happening in Kenya'.

Not surprisingly others disagreed, and the battle between the Church and natural family planning advocates on one hand, and organisations advocating the wider use of contraception, sterilisation and abortion on the other was a backdrop of many of the couples' encounters with medical staff in the third world. Religious ethics aside, the strong selling point of the Billings Method, provided husbands as well as wives would follow it, was that it was free and once understood, did not need medical follow-up.

More than a decade before the Rwandan civil war that began in 1990 and the genocide in which as many as 800,000 people were massacred over a three month period in 1994, John and Evelyn resurrected their long-ago French studies on that 1979 trip to talk to people in the central African country. "In the morning we went to Rutongo on a hill some distance from Kigali where a group of Belgian Sisters train young girls in needlework and provide an income for them by selling their beautiful products. There were more than 200 girls in the workrooms and they smiled pleasantly at us in the beautiful Rwandan way as we watched them carrying out their lovely handiwork."

John and Lyn with African baby

In the afternoon they visited the Medical School at Butare in the south of Rwanda, near the border with Burundi. Flying in a six-seater aircraft over some of the Rwandan hills, they arrived after a bumpy journey to be greeted by several hundred medical staff and students, who plied them with questions about what their method had to offer. Throughout Africa, the Method was taken up and taught by various local doctors and missionaries, including German-born Sister Brigitta Schnell, a missionary nun, who is also a physician and has devoted much of her working life to teaching it in Tanzania. In Nigeria, one of its leading proponents was Sister Leonie McSweeney, an Irish physician who qualified at University College Dublin and joined Mother Mary Martin's Medical Missionaries of Mary in 1951, before being assigned to Nigeria in 1960. Sister Leonie's study on the BOM and sex selection was published recently. In her efforts to apply the Method to sex selection, Sister Leonie was motivated by concerns that women who did not produce a male child were being banished from their tribal homes. The study is available on the Billings Ovulation Method website: http://www.thebillingsovulationmethod.org/articles

Bishop Fisher, for one, was not surprised by the Billings' success in Africa. "Obviously for countries without the money or ideological inclination to get tied into the globalised pharmacologizing of fertility, the availability of a practically free alternative is hugely attractive," he said. "In some cases these cultures are also more attuned to the cycles of the body anyway and so find the Method simpatico."

As on most trips, the three-week visit to Africa left little time for relaxation. Fortunately, their journey in Kenya took them through the National Park at Nakura, where they saw "water bucks, velvet monkeys, gazelles and giraffes, and, on the vast expanse of water, pelicans, flamingos" and other birds. The vegetation included Australian gum trees, wattle trees that were coming into bloom and "the acacia trees provide food for the giraffes – they are tall trees with horizontal branches, their light golden trunks giving them a rather ghostly appearance."

Eastern Europe, before the collapse of Communism, was also an eye-opener as John and Lyn heard one distressing story after another about life under Communist oppression as their hosts kept a wary eye out for secret police. For many citizens, the Billings discovered first hand, life under Soviet oppression amounted to "living within a police state, knowing that they were constantly being spied upon and possibly destined to be subjected to unjust accusations and condemnation, forced to endure low wages and difficult living conditions. Experiencing no reward at all for efforts to work hard for the good of the population at large, the people all tended to become dispirited. Feeling no loyalty or gratitude towards the Government they tended rather to try to cheat, so that at least some of their produce could be retained for their own benefit or at least denied to their oppressors."

From Lithuanians they learned that out of a population of three million, about 300,000 people were sent to Siberia where many died. Among them was a journalist whose daughter told Lyn and John that her mother spent 12 years in Siberia for

Lyn and John in Yugoslavia

suggesting in an article that the colour of the national flag be changed. Romanians attending one of their courses in Zagreb related how the sharing of needles in hospital had infected many children with AIDS during an immunisation program. During one of numerous visits to the region of the former Yugoslavia that is now Croatia, John and Lyn were interrogated by a hospital director who wanted to know why they were visiting in response to invitations from religious rather than medical groups. On that occasion, they had just arrived from Moscow and John was able to answer that their work was acceptable to people of all cultures and that they had come from the All-Union Research Centre for Maternal and Child Health Care in the Soviet Union. "One was conscious of the fact that this reply uprooted the questioner's 'middle stump'; it was important not to laugh at him," John wrote later. Across Eastern Europe, as people again learned to live in freedom after the fall of the Berlin Wall they found "the message of Christianity a real source of hope."

In the Middle East, with the assistance of local Christian communities, John and Lyn took the Method to Egypt and Israel. Boarding the El Al aircraft in Rome for Tel Aviv in 1990, they had been told to expect a long interrogation due to security reasons. Questioned at length about why they were going to the Holy Land, who had invited them and details of their itinerary, Lyn explained to the young woman asking the questions that they were going to teach a new method of family planning. After capturing her interest, another young woman joined in until both were satisfied they understood the Method very well, and Lyn gave them a copy of her instruction book. In and around Tel Aviv,

Bethlehem, Nazareth and Jerusalem they addressed medical gatherings, groups of engaged couples, university medical students and senior school students. They found that while little had been done in NFP in either Israel or Palestine, the groups they met were keen to have competent programs established.

Such a frenetic travel schedule posed difficulties for the doctors and for their family. On a not untypical day in central and South America in 1984, for instance, after a hectic series of meetings and workshops in the United States, Jamaica and Trinidad, John and Lyn began their day in Marxist-run Guyana before flying to the city of Manaus on the Black River in Brazil, encountering a four-hour delay in Boa Vista en route. After meetings with local hospital staff and medical researchers engaged in promoting the Ovulation Method and Mass at a local parish, the doctors spent the evening recording a television discussion program on which they faced questions from local health officials. John recorded in his account: "Our day having begun before 3am with two separate flights, we were wondering when the program began whether we would be able to stay awake until it was over." Both were 66 years old at the time. They were energised by the progress they encountered on each trip, including the local doctor who told the television program that night that he had taught the Ovulation Method to 860 couples in the "favelas" (slums) of Sao Paulo and that just three pregnancies had been observed among the group, a method-related pregnancy rate of less than 1 per cent. "This is being reported in El Salvador, in India and so on, with experience of very large numbers of couples, including a high proportion of illiterates and the poorest of the poor."

The following day was taken up with meetings with bishops, priests and sisters in the morning and with doctors and medical students in the afternoon. The day ended with a late supper at a restaurant that served fish from the Amazon River. Preparing and delivering hour-long lectures and answering questions, often through translators, was all in a day's work. So was pitching each presentation to the particular audience and negotiating with local church and health workers to establish a permanent structure for teaching the Ovulation Method in as many cities, hospitals, towns and rural communities as possible.

It wasn't all serious business, however. At one presentation in Jamaica on their 1984 visit, John recorded that "Lyn made a great hit by a role-play demonstration of menstrual cycles of varying length, using two girls in red dresses to mark the beginning and end of the cycle, various nuns in white for the fertile phase, Dr Kevin Hume in a peaked cap marking the peak and another doctor as "Mrs Ovulation". Some nuns with their blue veils marked the three days of change after the Peak. This whole display caused considerable amusement but was a very effective teaching exercise."

As John and Evelyn's ventures to remote corners of the globe gathered pace and the trips became longer, it's little wonder that their children, some of whom like many of their generation questioned the value of Natural Family Planning in the modern world, were concerned about their parents. John and Lyn were also working hard when they were at home in Melbourne earning a living. It would also have been un-natural if their family had not felt resentment at the rapacious demands of their parents' work, which John and Evelyn pursued with missionary zeal. From September to November 1989, for example, at the age of 71 they were on the road continually, moving from Japan and China to Poland and Austria then across the Atlantic to Canada and the US.

Their youngest daughter, Catherine, had been 10 when their parents made their first overseas working visit in 1969. Several of her siblings were young teenagers and several others were in the vital, final years of secondary school. John's personal accounts of their travels show they approached their work with single-minded dedication. The accounts of their visits to different countries written by John contained few personal or family references but those included were always warm. In the Philippines in October 1988 they received "news of the premature arrival of our 28th grandchild, Paul David Reynolds, the fifth surviving child of our daughter Helen who had had a difficult time ending in a Caesarean Section; labour had begun prematurely at 33 weeks. After a few anxious days all had gone well and we were looking forward eagerly to be reunited with our family. Deo gratias."

During the visit to Macau and China in June and July 1998 he noted: "Today it happens to be the birthday of our beloved twins, Helen and Ruth. Ruth is now in Heaven and helping us along the way." He went on to describe how he had explained to somebody he had met that Christ's wounds "had been caused by the nails when he was crucified, but that he had risen from the dead afterwards."

It was around that time, when John and Lyn were 80, that

one of their children felt too upset to join in a toast at a gala dinner in Melbourne given in their honour and attended by Church dignitaries and a large number of supporters when it was announced that John and Lyn had decided to continue travelling "for another three years".

If anything, the schedule intensified, albeit briefly. At the age of 82 in 2000, John and Evelyn ventured to Rome and the Holy Land in February, to China in May, to the Philippines in June, back to Rome in September and again to China in October and November. Wherever they travelled, they were acutely aware of the struggles and sufferings they encountered, but also of the cheerfulness and vitality of so many different cultures. John wrote after leaving South America in 1984: "Each location we visited presented its own challenge, with uncertainty as to what might be encountered before the assignment was finished. We enjoyed many wonderful experiences and ... outstanding enrichment."

By that stage, John and Lyn were widely regarded as part of the 'aristocracy' of Melbourne's lively, pro-active Catholic tribe. They were regarded, as Bishop Fisher recalled, as the kindly old grandparents of Catholic medicine, doing a good job of encouraging the next generation, still with very sharp minds and enormously respected:

> Indeed, they were formidable. I remember having a difference of opinion with John about some point – it was a matter in which I agreed with his position personally, but felt I had to say that the Church had not spoken authoritatively on the matter and so people of well-informed conscience might go either way. John pulled my

piece from his publication: I've not often been accused of being too liberal!

I also saw them at meetings of the Pontifical Academy for Life in Rome, to which they were papal appointees. I'm not sure that people outside the natural family planning and bioethics world appreciated just how important they had been – partly because much of their work was done overseas. I remember at one time that some lay people were promoting the idea that John and Lyn be nominated for a Nobel Prize in Medicine. Several medical professors thought their contribution would have merited it. But their work was in such a controversial area, and Australian government policy so pro-contraception, that it was agreed that it was a no-goer.

There was no doubt that in John and Evelyn's minds, and those of their supporters who donated decades of their lives to assisting them and many more who supported their work financially, that the Billings were using their talents to the utmost to do the work of God. They often spoke of the BOM as "a message of Truth and Love."

In a speech delivered on Evelyn's behalf to a conference in Rome in 2008 to mark the 40th anniversary of *Humanae Vitae* about the cultural value of natural family planning she told participants:

> The blessings of Truth are constantly apparent to teachers of the Billings Ovulation Method. In January of this year, we began a teaching program in Vietnam. In preparing this paper we received the glad news of two new pregnancies achieved by couples who had suffered from the pain of infertility. One for 17 years and the other for 8 years.[1]

John's writings also reveal the strength of the faith that drove him and Evelyn in their work, with the diary entries peppered with references to "the abundant blessings which the Father of us all in Heaven has showered upon this work, and which He will continue to bless if we all continue to pray hard enough and to work hard enough."

John amd Lyn with a large group of Italian teachers.
Dr (Sr) Anna Cappella is on Lyn's left

1. http://www.woombinternational.org/philosophy/the-cultural-value-of-natural-family-planning.html

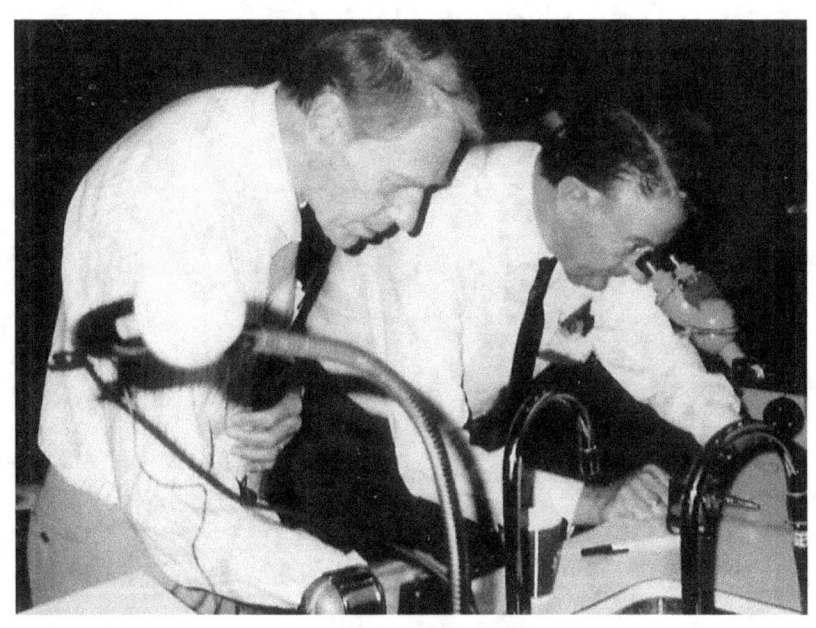

Professor Erik Odeblad and Dr John Billings view mucus samples

6
The Research Stacks Up

As the Billings' travels progressed, their message was strengthened by the results of a series of clinical trials that consolidated the reputation of the Method and attracted generous private donations in Australia and overseas.

The World Health Organisation recognised Lyn's expertise in 1981 when she served as a member of an expert committee on natural family planning at a WHO meeting in Geneva. Her own contribution to the science of the Method related to the Basic Infertile Pattern and the Method's usefulness for pre-menopausal and breast-feeding women.

News of the first official clinical trial of the Billings Ovulation Method had been published in *The Lancet* in October 1972. The trial involved a group of 282 Tongan women, spread over many islands, who were introduced to the Method by a missionary nun of the Marist Order, Sister Cosmas Weissmann, who had visited Melbourne in search of a simple and reliable method of family planning for her people. Sister Cosmas spent several weeks learning the Method from Lyn and how to teach it, before returning to Tonga and passing on the knowledge to more than 300 women who wanted to postpone pregnancy.

The Trial, conducted from July 1970 to January 1972, found that three pregnancies occurred among the 282 couples participating, with the nun keeping meticulous records. Two of the pregnancies were attributed to teacher error and one to method failure, although it was later revealed by one of the couples, after publication of the Lancet study, that they had been aware of fertile signs and had decided they were happy to conceive a child. The trial also established that the Method was simple to teach and easily understood.[1]

Further trials followed. One of the largest was conducted simultaneously in India, The Philippines, El Salvador, New Zealand and Ireland from 1976 to 1978, and overseen by the World Health Organisation. Again the results were impressive. Among 869 couples monitored over 10,215 monthly cycles, the pregnancy rate due to Method failure was 2.9 per cent. The pregnancy rate attributed to teaching errors was 3.9 per cent.[2]

But a larger trial in the United States that ran from 1975 to 1977 involving 1090 couples over 12,282 monthly cycles attending six clinics promoting the Billings Ovulation Method produced a pregnancy rate of just one per cent due to Method failure and none due to teaching failure.[3]

The dissemination of the Method in the US owed much to a specialist obstetrician/gynaecologist, Dr Hanna Klaus, a member of the Medical Mission Sisters. In 2008, in a speech at St Louis University, Dr Klaus recalled the impact of a book on natural family planning she received while working as a physician at Washington University. The book was a guide to the Billings Method, a gift from Cardinal John Carberry to Catholic doctors.

Most threw it in the trash. But I didn't. It was the beginning of a long journey learning much more about not only the medical, but the personal and spiritual aspects of conjugal love. ...

There is no justification for using a powerful drug which may have undesirable short or long-term consequences, just to isolate a normal function from the body ... when people tell you (NFP) doesn't work, tell them you have different information. When we stop trying to separate sex from procreation, our society will stop trying to arrest psychosexual maturation at the level of early adolescence. We can then hope to have a society composed of adults who know how to delay gratification and accept responsibility for their actions.[4]

John and Lyn were also keen supporters of Dr Klaus's initiative, the TeenSTAR (Sexuality Teaching in the context of Adult Responsibility) movement, which has spread to 30 countries. TeenSTAR is a developmental curriculum which informs teenagers about fertility patterns and teaches responsible decision-making and communication skills in sexual behaviour.

Other trials, which produced remarkably consistent results, were conducted in Australia, Africa, India and Indonesia.[5] In India, couples taught the Method by Missionaries of Charity sisters, the order founded by Mother Teresa, achieved a 99.4% effectiveness rate in a World Health Organization study.[6]

Mother Teresa and her Missionaries of Charity were keen advocates of the Billings Ovulation Method from shortly after its inception, with numerous Sisters trained by Lyn in Melbourne before they travelled to Calcutta or other destinations.

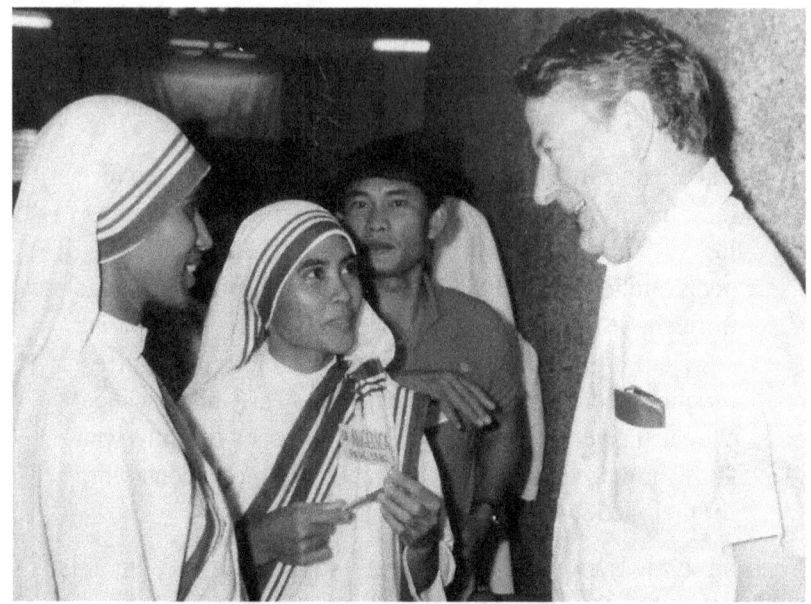

John Billings with two Missionaries of Charity

At the 1978 Conference organised by the John and Lyn in Melbourne, to celebrate the 10th Anniversary of the publication of *Humanae Vitae,* Mother Teresa revealed that in Calcutta alone, her sisters had taught over 12,000 couples to use the BOM. Later, during a time when sterilisation was heavily promoted in India, Mother Teresa went to the Government and proved that on a natural basis alone, with the help of BOM and her sisters, they could assist in preventing the birth of 30,000 fewer babies in three years. The Government formally recognised such work.

John and Lyn made 11 trips to India over 25 years, from 1974 onwards, where the Method also received strong backing from Sister Catherine Bernard, a medical doctor and member of the French order the Sisters of the Cross. Sister Catherine established and operates two family life centres – one at Tiruchirapalli in the Tamil region of southern India and the Service and Research Institute of Family and Children (SERFAC) at Chennai in southeast India. In their usual hands-on style, Lyn and John Billings worked extensively with both orders to establish a foothold for the Method in a nation where natural family planning had previously been largely unknown. This was in spite of the fact that in 1983, the Catholic Church was running about 23 per cent of hospitals, although only about two per cent of the population were Catholic. Both orders of nuns are continuing to promulgate the Billings Ovulation Method in the 21st century.

In a 2007 interview with Catholic News Asia Sister Catherine Bernard recalled John and Lyn, who knew of her work, seeking

In Madras, India

her out when they first visited India, when she was teaching natural family planning in rural villages: "Doctor Billings and his wife influenced me tremendously and profoundly," Sister Catherine recalled. "As a couple, they themselves were witnesses to the truth. They were an example of genuine family love and love for humanity. Their life motivated me. In them, I found concrete expressions of God's love for people. I said, 'There has to be some good about it,' and I continue to discover that good'."[7]

From her observations, it was clear that the Method could help keep a marriage together.

> Husband and wife learn to respect each other and their fertility. They begin to respect their combined fertility. Periodic abstinence makes their marriage stronger. Children become gifts of marriage. They begin to be life-givers in society. As far as I am aware, it has no drawbacks, but there are two difficulties. One is that people have to maintain a chart. Some people find it cumbersome. The second is that its promotion is slow. We have to move from person to person, couple to couple, and follow it up.

At that time, Sister Catherine commented,

> [A]t least 73 percent of Indians do not use any contraceptives, according to researched and proven data. Many do not use contraceptives simply because they do not like it. Some use herbs or the rhythm method. Most don't use the Billings method because no one has taught them about it. A larger number of people would use it if they knew about it.
>
> Everyone along the ladder, from highest official to seminarian, needs to be educated about the truth of natural family planning, and the Billings method. They should

become convinced about it. You can't teach something you're not convinced of. Then we need to invest money, time and resources. Get as much manpower, including laypeople, train them and send out like apostles. But you also have to see to their maintenance.[8]

An article published by the US-based National Center for Biotechnology Information in 1993 reached a similar conclusion. It reported that the Ovulation Method proved acceptable to a sample group of 501 women, half urban based and half rural based, who had previously either shunned contraception or relied on condoms. The authors, G. Sinha and A. Sinha of the Department of Obstetrics and Gynaecology, Nalanda Medical College Hospital, Patna concluded: "Women who shun contraception, often due to fear of side-effects, do accept

John and Lyn at a conference in India, 1997

simple, safe, and effective BOM. Workers who are already promoting maternal and child health services can be trained to train women about BOM without spending more money to hire BOM trainers.'"[9]

A more recent trial involving 2059 women in India over 21 months resulted in a pregnancy rate of .86 per cent among women wanting to avoid pregnancy.[8] Disturbed by the increasing incidence of induced abortion in India, Mother Teresa wrote to Lyn and John Billings in early 1995, inviting them to work more closely with her sisters to spread knowledge of the Method. When they arrived in Calcutta, Mother Teresa, by then very frail and protected from the crowds who flocked around her at morning Mass, asked them to concentrate on teaching a group of 70 new sisters who were completing their training.

John wrote in his diary:

> From now on each day we went to the Park Street House of the Missionaries. It proved to be a very energetic, enthusiastic and happy group of trainees who co-operated actively in responding to the instruction and in carrying out the various tasks set for them as 'homework'. Mother Teresa stayed for the whole of the session on the first day and was very pleased with the interest immediately displayed by the sisters under instruction. After they have been professed in May a few of them will remain to work in different places in India and the rest will be sent all around the world in 123 countries.

Mother Teresa told Lyn and John extraordinary stories of her experiences – of the home for prostitutes she had rescued from jail and who had been disowned by their families; of the beggar who approached her in a Calcutta street to give her his few coins, which she accepted for fear of offending him and how his eyes became radiant when she accepted; and the young girl, given to Mother Teresa by her birth mother, to be adopted and who returned to the convent immediately after marrying to adopt a child herself "saying she owed such a gift to God, before she and her husband tried to have children themselves."

As well as instructing the sisters, the Billings' work in India involved teaching hospital staff and non-government health workers, each one of whom was responsible for caring for two or three villages of up to 10,000 people. While poverty remained a serious problem at that time, there were also signs that India was slowly developing economically and that hunger and disease were on the wane.

In Italy, the leader in promoting the Billings Ovulation Method was Dominican Sister and medical doctor, Anna Cappella, whose collaboration with John and Lyn began in 1972 when she was working as a missionary and gynaecologist in Pakistan at St. Dominic's Hospital, Bahawalpur and was treating women for whom pregnancy was difficult because of poverty, poor health and environmental conditions. Dr Cappella, who had undertaken her medical training in New York, regarded the Method as "an extraordinary answer to the women's and their families' conditions, as an instrument of knowledge, prevention and promotion of human dignity …To educate means to let people know what is inside nature."[10]

After teaching the Method to local women, Dr Cappella was recalled to Rome by the Italian Bishops' Conference to work in tertiary education. There she taught and promoted the BOM in her roles as Director of the Family Counselling Centre at the Faculty of Medicine of the Gemelli Hospital, and at the Centre for Study and Research on Natural Fertility Regulation which she founded at the Catholic University of the Sacred Heart in Rome. There she assembled a group of doctors and staff to promote the Method – work that drew the warm approval of Pope John Paul II. Dr Cappella also became one of the foundational teachers at the John Paul II Institute for the Family at the Lateran University.

In April 2009, after Dr Cappella's death, Lyn Billings recalled their first meeting in Karachi:

> Sr Anna seized the method and began teaching, realising its value in enriching marriages and families with generosity, truth and love. She set about inspiring others to train others to teach, thus protecting them from the damaging programs imposed upon them.
>
> Gradually Anna's worth was recognised to have special qualities and she was directed to go to Rome to set up a Centre there, to teach and particularly to contact and train missionary sisters who were constantly passing through Rome. She attracted and gathered around her a remarkable, capable and devoted band of Italian women – doctors, sisters and mothers. Inspired by her staunch goodness and gentle care Anna extended her influence far and wide in Italy and later to other parts of Europe, Africa, Latin America including Cuba, Lebanon and the Holy Land. Sr Anna attended many BOM Conferences recording every word and producing very valuable Italian materials.
>
> It was a great sacrifice for Anna to give up her missionary work in Pakistan, but as usual following the call of Truth and

Love, great things have been done. Firm friendships have been developed and still endure as a result of her travels, conferences, books and videos and in her insistence on orthodoxy of the Method. Her gentle goodness emanated from her unshakeable Faith.

We are proud to be part of an estimable group of devoted teachers who loved working with Anna and enjoyed her

Lyn with a copy of her book at Human Life International in Washington, 1981

surety and grace. She will live on in Truth and Love and in our gratitude.

Throughout the world, news of the Billings Ovulation Method and a detailed, step-by-step guide on how to follow it were set out in a book that was first published in 1980 which has since sold more than one million copies in 22 languages. *The Billings Method: Controlling Fertility without Drugs or Devices* was written by Dr Evelyn Billings and Dr Ann Westmore, a Melbourne scientist and historian. After its initial appearance it was reprinted in 1980 and 1981 published in paperback in 1982 and reprinted at least once a year until 1987. A new edition was published in 1988 and reprinted and revised 11 times until 2006. After a complete rewrite in 2011 to make the material more accessible to general readers, it was republished as *The Billings Method: Using the Body's Natural Signal of Fertility to Achieve or Avoid Pregnancy* by Anne O'Donovan and distributed by Penguin. Royalties from the book have been a major funding source for the promulgation of the Billings Ovulation Method globally.

In Brazil, its widespread acceptance owed much to the tireless work of Sister Martha Silvia Bhering, a teacher and nurse who joined the Society of the Daughters of Charity of St. Vincent de Paul in 1940. Her work as an obstetrics nurse in Sao Paulo and Rio de Janeiro brought her into contact with pregnant women from all areas of society, including the poorest of the poor. On learning of the Billings Ovulation Method in 1973, she realised "that this was a method of the couple that invited the effective participation of man, setting women free from dependence on resources outside their own nature and physiology."[11] From that point, while recognising that the Method was "swimming against the tide" in the modern world, BOM study groups and teaching became her life's mission, which she pursued from one end of Brazil to the other until her death at the age of 91.

1. M.C. Weissman, J. Folaiki, E.L. Billings, J.J. Billings, "A trial of the Ovulation Method of family planning in Tonga", *Lancet*, 813-16, 14 October, 1972. Reported on the WOOMB website: http://www.woomb.org/bom/trials/index.html Retrieved 30 March 2012.

2. World Health Organisation, Task Force on Methods for the Determination of the Fertile Period, Special Programme of Research, Development and Research Training in Human Reproduction, "A Prospective Multicentre Trial of the Ovulation Method of Natural Family Planning, I, The Teaching Phase", *Fertility and Sterility*, 36.152, 1981.

3. H. Klaus et al., "Use effectiveness and client satisfaction in six centres teaching the Billings Ovulation Method", *Contraception*, 19:6, 613, 1979.

4. http://vox-nova.com/2008/08/16/dr-hanna-klaus-on-humanae-vitae/

5. http://www.woomb.org/bom/trials/index.html Retrieved March 30th 2012

6. http://www.dcfl.org/NaturalFamilyPlanning/billings.asp

7. http://www.catholic.org/international/international_story.php?id=24941&page=1

8. http://www.ncbi.nlm.nih.gov/pubmed/8308307

9. http://www.woomb.org/bom/lit/afp.shtml

10. *History of the development and growth of the Billings Ovulation Method™ in Italy* by Paola Pellicano, 26 September 2011.

11. Paper on Sister Martha Silvia Bhering by Heloisa Pereira President, CENPLAFAM-WOOMB Brazil

Australian teachers and China team, back row, L-R, Marian Corkill, Professor Qian Shao-Zhen, Dr Evelyn Billings, Dr John Billings, Marie Marshell; front row, L-R, Kerry Bourke, Merilyn Kennealy, Professor Qian's wife Rosie, Gillian Barker

7
Coal, Iron Ore and Natural Family Planning

As she grasped their hands in gratitude, her eyes full of tears, the Chinese family planning teacher's hands were noticed by the Billings team from Australia to be hard and calloused from prolonged manual labour. Like many of her compatriots in the late 1980s, she had done her share of farm labouring and wielding a pick and shovel on the roads. Her message, conveyed through a translator was clear: "Thank you. I've had eight abortions and now I know my daughter will never have to go through the same." It was a familiar story, repeated many times all over China by different women in the late 1980s as the Billings Ovulation Method began to make its mark.

Motivated by a desire to help Chinese families deal with the state's harsh one-child policy in the midst of poverty, John Billings wrote to the Chinese Government in 1985, offering to travel to China to introduce the Ovulation Method. The timing of the request was auspicious, because despite stringent contraceptive and abortion programs, population growth remained a serious problem in China. By that time, the Chinese Government, through the World Health Organisation, was exploring the availability of an effective natural method.

Before the industrial revolution that was to transform China into an economic powerhouse had begun to gather pace, fuelling an unprecedented resources boom in Australia in the first decades of the 21th century, John and Evelyn made their first visit to China in July 1986. They met members of the State Family Planning Commission, the body which oversaw the national programs.

They found widespread poverty, dissatisfaction with state-run family planning and a people who detested the memory of Stalin, whose extreme cruelty they abhorred. At the same time, many referred to the Communist Party's 1949 victory as the "war of liberation". On their first visit, the doctors were given approval to lecture on their work in Beijing, Shanghai and Nanjing. In Shanghai, they met a leading andrologist, Professor

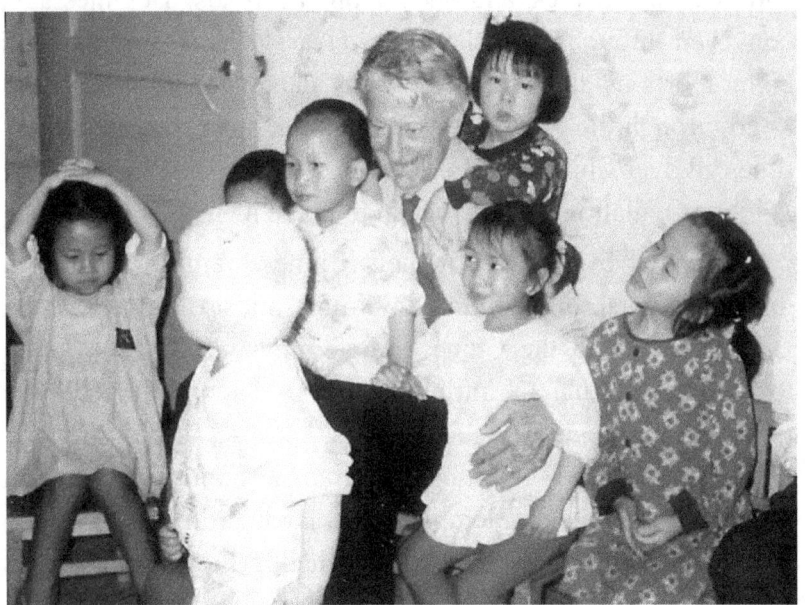

John with Chinese orphans at the House of Love in Kunming, 1997

Qian Shao-Zhen, a WHO member who recognised the potential of their work. "This method would be good for China. I would like to help you," he said.

He did, inviting them to attend further conferences, as they established the Billings Ovulation Method in Nanjing and neighbouring provinces. Evelyn recalled: "He wanted to help because he knew that the current program of fertility regulation was not working well and because he had a great love of his fellow Chinese." While not a Christian, Shao-Zhen, who spoke excellent English, was a graduate of the Pennsylvanian Medical School in the US and St John's University in Nanjing, which before the Cultural Revolution functioned under the direction of the Anglican Church. It was there that he met his wife, Rosie, who graduated in biology in 1947 and who later helped with translating some of the Billings teaching materials.

Early on the doctors were asked: "What do you do about the pregnancies?" They would have no part of abortion, understanding better than most the miracle of early foetal development and the fact that within a month of conception, the infant's heart is beating. Evelyn recalled:

> We knew we would have to teach well to avoid pregnancies that would be terminated. Fortunately, the Australian teachers have been excellent and have been inspired by a respect and love for these people. The Chinese teachers have responded wholeheartedly with confidence in the reliability of a thoroughly verified scientific method and they are very conscientious and meticulous.

As John Billings noted during a visit to China in August

1996, some Chinese health professionals were sceptical about whether husbands would co-operate with the restraint demanded by the Billings Ovulation Method. In practice, the teachers found that husbands and wives would come together for the first instruction, and if the husbands had major objections they were not raised. John observed on one visit: "Lyn always talks a lot to these trainees about the conjugal relationship and we try to help them understand how living the BOM in married life teaches the husband and wife to love one another."

In an interview at home in Shanghai in 2010, Professor Shao-Zhen recalled that John Billings arrived in China in 1986 complete with teaching materials and charts for the Method, which were quickly snapped up by members of the audience, especially the large numbers of female gynaecologists. "I had hundreds of women chasing me for more material," Professor Shao-Zhen recalled. The materials were quickly translated and for use not only in China but in Hong Kong, Malaysia and Singapore."

From the outset, the Billings' efforts were assisted by a group of young, enthusiastic women from Caritas (the Catholic aid agency) in Hong Kong, whose fluency in Mandarin, Cantonese and local dialects made them invaluable translators. After learning the method, the group also established BOM centres in Hong Kong and Macau.

Over the next 14 years the doctors and their team, including senior Billings Method teachers from Melbourne visited China two or three times a year, for three weeks at a time. In boiling summers and freezing winters, the small teams traversed much of

John and Lyn with Chinese woman

China, from the Pacific coast to inner Mongolia. They travelled for hundreds of kilometres over bumpy roads in primitive vehicles and trucks, sometimes with livestock and chickens on board and were buoyed by the enthusiasm with which they were welcomed, including by the officials and Communist Party minders who kept an eye on them. They stayed in hospitals and very basic hotels but found their hosts warm and hospitable.

Marie Marshell, the senior teacher who accompanied the doctors on every visit to China but one recalls that their reception was always "incredibly positive", with the gatherings of medical staff and family planners they addressed inevitably packed out, even in the most remote centres. At each gathering, it was easy to identify which family planning officials were

John and Lyn in China with Australian teachers and translators from Caritas

most receptive and who would begin teaching others to teach the method. "There was a ripple effect like a pebble," Marie Marshell recalled. "Each one would tell five or 10 people and they would teach another five or 10 people and the Method became incorporated in family planning clinics." At a time when many Chinese women performed heavy manual labour, some found they preferred a natural method to the bleeding, pain and infection that sometimes went with the IUD, as well as the problems of expulsion that many women found with the device.

Typical of the hundreds of gatherings John and Lyn addressed in China was one attended by 500 gynaecologists and a few nurses in 1990 in Nanjing, then a smoggy city of about three million people. Through translators, they outlined the Ovulation Method and were encouraged by the interest of their audience, who, through two translators, clamoured for more information and supplies of teaching literature. The supplies ran out fast. In a Communist nation where Christian religion was marginalised and abortions forced upon women whether they wanted them or not, Catholic sensibilities about contraception as opposed to natural family planning barely registered a blip in China. And without the backing of the Catholic Church the Billings Ovulation Method enjoyed in Melbourne, it had to stand on its efficacy alone among the Chinese. In some ways, this was its ultimate test. It passed with flying colours. In 1995, Australia's aid agency AusAID provided funding for a three-year project in Anhui Province, a breakthrough that saw John, Evelyn, Marie Marshell and other teachers covering 4,000km through industrial and agricultural regions.

The following year, Chinese authorities embarked on one of the best-designed and most rigorous independent evaluations of the Method when 1,654 healthy married women of proven-fertility (having at least one live birth), aged 24-35 years, with regular menstrual cycles were enrolled with the support of their husbands. The participants were mostly peasants, but some were white collar workers with different levels of education. They were randomly divided in the ratio of 3 to 2 into two groups (the BOM group had 992 subjects and the IUD group had 662 subjects). The observation was continued for 12 months. John, Lyn and their team were not informed of progress and had to wait until the final results. These showed that in the BOM group, five women became pregnant due to user-error of the Method. In contrast, the smaller IUD group had 12 pregnancies, and another 15 women expelled the device and it had to be removed from 38 others for medical reasons, mainly because of severe side-effects. The Chinese authorities were sufficiently convinced by these results, and the method was adopted officially by the Chinese Ministry of Health as one of the approved choices for fertility regulation.

On his eighth visit to China in 1996, John Billings noted that he found "obstinate resistance" by doctors to natural family planning was "much smaller" there than elsewhere. "Another extraordinary observation that we have made consistently in our eight visits to China so far is that despite all their suffering, and especially the suffering of the women, the Chinese people are brave, happy, lovable people who have accepted us and our teaching with great friendliness and obviously love their children very deeply."

In a return visit later that year researchers at the Institute of Reproductive Medicine research in Wuhu in the south-eastern Anhui province reported that the pregnancy rate among users of the IUD in the province was at least 14 per cent higher than among women following the Billings Method. Enthusiasm for the BOM teaching project that Lyn, John, Marie Marshell and Merilyn Kennealy encountered on their trip in November 1996 was indicative of how keenly the Method was embraced in China. They found that since their previous visit seven months earlier, 600 additional teachers had been trained in the province, and 27 seminars conducted in six cities of the province – Hefei the capital, Wuhu, Beng-Bu, Tong Ling, Huang Shan (Yellow

Mountain) and Xuan-Cheng – which were home to 13 million out of 60 million in the province. In turn, each teacher had been given the target by Chinese medical authorities of training at least 20 new teachers per month, with their performances assessed by more senior teachers. Particular efforts were made for every teacher to instruct at least 10 couples or women about to be married during every three-month period.

In a paper given at Melbourne University in March 2003 at the International Jubilee Conference to mark the 50th anniversary of the Billings Method, Qian Shao-Zhen updated delegates on progress of the Method in China. By that stage, he said, "fourteen BOM Centres have been established in China at the most strategic areas for fertility regulation and 36,845 Billings Ovulation Method teachers have been trained. A certain percentage of the teachers were trained by the Australian Teaching Group led by Drs JJ and EL Billings. Up to date the method has been regularly used by more than 2,686,400 fertile couples for avoiding pregnancy, the overall success rate being around 99%; In addition, there were 14,524 among 45,280 infertile couples (success rate 32.1%) who were overjoyed to obtain their children by the use of BOM.

"The common people affectionately called these kids the Billings babies." And the doctors in charge of the Billings Infertility Clinics in China have been given the title "Baby-Provider". Understanding of the Method, the Professor said, had also prompted many women to consult gynaecologists for early diagnosis and treatment, when they observed abnormal symptoms.[1]

"The BOM results in China exerted a big impact on both the Chinese community and the medical circle and there were 48 papers, broadcasting stations, TV stations and five journals

Professor Qian Shao-Zhen and Dr John Billings in China

reported the news of Drs J.J. and E.L. Billings and their wonderful method," Professor Qian said. "In most provinces, the BOM has already been incorporated into the Government Family Planning Programme as one of the methods of choice by the fertile couples.

"The method is highly efficient only when a series of precautions and regulations are strictly followed. Inappropriate use would result in higher failure rates, as in preliminary trials in China (1989) and some other places. Drawing a lesson from the early work, we always stick to the authenticated Billings teaching materials. In China only the authenticated BOM materials (Chinese translation, with the approval of WOOMB) are used and nobody is permitted to rewrite, revise or modify them. In China, the BOM book, booklet, wall charts, slide rule, etc. are among the most popular reference materials for family planning. We also provide these materials to Chinese-speaking peoples outside China.

"We pay much attention to the teacher-training course and the women-teaching course, as well as an adequate guidance system and regular follow-up visits to the couples. Such a programme not only imparts scientific knowledge but also provokes and maintains the initiative of the women and their husbands, who are invited to participate in every other follow-up interview. Qualified teachers, the acquisition of BOM knowledge by the participants, the women's motivation and the husbands' cooperation are the key points for the successful implementation of BOM."

Use of the Method, Professor Qian said, had not only

brought about a decrease in the birth rate among fertile couples, but had caused a significant decrease in the abortion rate. "In Community A of one municipality, the BOM was widely spread, the yearly artificial abortion rate in 2002 being 0.61% (per 100 fertile women), while in the neighbouring Community B, where BOM was seldom used, the rate was 4.06%. which was almost 7 times that of A, the difference being highly significant. The basic conditions of the two communities were similar and their artificial abortion rates in the past had been also similar."

It is a measure of how rapidly the Method was accepted in China that by the end of 2003 it was being used by 3,645,600 fertile couples for avoiding pregnancy _ an increase of almost a million couples in nine months. They had been taught the Method by 48,449 Chinese teachers, who in turn had been instructed by 1871 core-teachers trained by Billings staff from Australia.[2]

For John and Evelyn, one of the main motivations behind their back-breaking work in many cities and rural corners of China was to relieve the suffering they encountered that came from compulsory abortion and inadequate contraceptive programs. As they described it in 1996: "The people are living in a police state and they live in fear, because they are the subjects of a brutal government which enforced its decisions through very severe punitive measures for those who disobey.

"It is very interesting to observe their reaction when you speak during the course of a lecture about love, happiness, security and peace within the family. They are quiet during the lecture and during this time a kind of stillness becomes evident, indicating not tension but attention. They stare at us and listen and sometimes a close observer can see a tear running down a cheek."

In Bishop Anthony Fisher's view, the success of the Billings Method in preventing millions of abortions in China has been "a huge achievement". He also suspects that "it also gradually changes attitudes to the body, the need for males and females to understand and co-operate with each other's bodies and their attitudes to children. So what the Chinese and others go into merely as a "method" to avoid pregnancy may actually open their eyes to the goodness of fertility and children."

These days, teaching and promotion of the Billings Ovulation Method in China is centred in China, headquartered at the Nanjing Billings Natural Fertility Regulation Research Centre of Excellence in Nanjing and with several support centres throughout the country. The transition to Chinese control was one which John and Evelyn Billings long planned over several visits, in conjunction with local medical authorities and supporters. Leaders of the Chinese program remain in close contact with the Billings organisation in Melbourne.

The Chinese government officially recognised the Billings'contribution with a Distinctive Contribution Award from the Consultation Committee of the Ministry of Health. They were also appointed honorary advisors to the Beijing, Shanghai and Nanjing Family Planning Commissions.

1. http://www.woomb.org/bom/trials/chinaLaunching.html
2. Ibid 8. *Bulletin.* p. 22, March 2004.

www.thebillingsovulationmethod.org – official website 2013

8
Now and Into the Future

Members of the UN General Assembly gained an insight into the relevance of the Billings Method in Western nations in the 21st century at a Special Session on population and development in late June and early July 1999. Addressing the Assembly, Susan Fryer, a Canadian staffer from the World Organization Ovulation Method Billings (WOOMB International) revealed that the organisation's website had 311,000 visits in March that year, compared with 30,000 visits during the same month the previous year: "Most of the visitors came from the U.S.A. and the E.U. and had selected 'achieve pregnancy' as their reason for wanting to use the method."[1]

Evelyn Billings developed the same theme in an article in WOOMB's regular bulletin in November 2009.

> In many centres around the world where the Billings Ovulation Method is taught, a majority of the couples presenting for instruction come for assistance in achieving a pregnancy," she said. "This was not so much the case in the past and is perhaps a measure of the rising infertility in the community, but it is also a recognition that natural methods of regulating fertility can be of great assistance in this regard.
>
> It is estimated that approximately 20 per cent of couples

trying to have a child are unable to do so. Yet most couples are unprepared for infertility and unaware that in many cases it can be overcome naturally by recourse to the time of optimum fertility in the cycle. Infertility is usually defined as the inability to conceive after 12 to 18 months of sexual intercourse without contraception. Apparent infertility may be caused by physical and/or psychological factors. Some of the contributing physical factors could be the age of the couple, particularly of the woman, whether either of them smokes tobacco or marijuana, if the woman is under or overweight, previous contraceptive use, illness, infection and damage to the reproductive organs. Some of the psychological factors may include stress perhaps from overwork, anxiety about money or other problems, or tension, fear or guilt – perhaps the couple blaming one another for the inability to conceive. Over-rigorous athletic training can inhibit ovulation temporarily.[2]

Bishop Fisher believes that the discovery of the Billings Ovulation Method has been providential because it provides a natural way of approaching both spacing of children responsibly and dealing with apparent infertility. He commented:

> With infertility at epidemic proportions in the West at present it is remarkable that more attention is not being given to natural responses. I've often heard of couples who were rushed into IVF programmes *before* the causes of their infertility had been investigated or the natural responses tried.
>
> Then after many failed attempts at IVF and having given up on ever getting pregnant, they've conceived naturally ... I've also had couples whom IVF clinics have told it was hopeless or would require many intrusive and expensive

IVF cycles speak to me. Having referred them to the Billings team they've conceived a child. Naprotechnology and other applications of the Method to achieve pregnancy as much as to avoid it help to underline that it is a very different thing to contraception. No one ever heard of infertile people using the Pill as a way to help them conceive!

Changing social patterns that have seen couples marrying later and the numbers of women attempting to become pregnant in their late 30s and 40s increasing have transformed the work of WOOMB International, especially in Australia. The support of a good teacher, Evelyn wrote in 2009, was invaluable to couples wanting to conceive. By 2012, about 80 per cent of calls to the BOM headquarters in Melbourne were from women all over the world seeking advice about how to boost their chances of becoming pregnant without resorting to the difficulties and expense of IVF, a process that unfortunately destroys many embryos for every one that is brought to term.

WOOMB charges such individuals and couples about $150. A five-year study on use of the Billings method recorded a 78.3 per cent success rate, including 35 per cent for women who had previously had IVF or assisted reproductive technology (ART). The average time from initial instruction to conception was 4.7 months. Of the 384 couples, 207 (54 per cent) had known infertility factors; the confirmed pregnancy rate in this group was 65 per cent. In women over 38 years of age the success rate of the BOM team in helping them to conceive was 66 per cent, with more than nine out of 10 agreeing the Method had given them an understanding of fertility and infertility and a similar percentage saying they would be happy to recommend it to others.

Marian Corkill, Director of WOOMB International, told *The Daily Telegraph* in 2009 that in an initial consultation for infertility "we explain the basis of the Billings method and get women to chart their cervical mucus on a daily basis ... After two weeks, they come back and we follow through until the end of their chart. Charting also means we can see what's normal and what's not. If anything is amiss, we'll advise the patient to go for tests."

Melbourne General Practitioner Dr Mary Walsh, who is a qualified BOM teacher and lecturer at the John Paul II Institute for Marriage and the Family, opened a Fertility Assessment Clinic at her practice in early 2012. Within the first few months, she was able with the help of the BOM to diagnose hypothyroidism, a pituitary tumour and polycystic ovarian syndrome in three of her patients attending the clinic.

Dr Walsh believes that increased fertility awareness is vital at a time when infertility is becoming more of a problem, especially among couples who are delaying starting a family. "Couples could save themselves a lot of time and heartache by trying a natural method first but unfortunately, for many people, their first referral while struggling to become pregnant is to an IVF clinic," she said.

She acknowledges that many doctors and patients remain sceptical about such a natural method for preventing or improving the chances of pregnancy. She has noticed it is becoming better accepted, however, in treating infertility and sub-fertility and believes the BOM is more likely to receive mainstream acceptance for that purpose than for preventing pregnancy. Not only does it allow women trying to conceive to maximise their chances by identifying their most fertile days, it can help doctors uncover medical conditions that are contributing to infertility or sub-fertility.

Dr Walsh participates in several forums for medical practitioners run by WOOMB every year in Melbourne on the clinical applications of the BOM. She has found the feedback "excellent". Similar information sessions are held in all states. As a medical practitioner, she finds it "logical" to encourage patients to take advantage of their "natural, built-in fertility marker". She admits that while some patients are "slightly fearful" of being without the Pill when they do not want to become pregnant, others have changed their minds after experiencing its side-effects.

In a 1998 article in *The Australian Family Physician* co-authored with ethicist Nicholas Tonti-Filippini, Dr Walsh cited a 1995 Commonwealth Department of Human Services and Health survey to determine the use of contraceptive methods in Australia by women and men between the ages of 15 and 54 years:

> Asked which methods they had ever used, 25 per cent said that they had used periods of abstinence/celibacy, 10 per cent the rhythm method, and 7 per cent the Billings Ovulation Method (BOM).
>
> It would appear from this that a significant proportion of people surveyed had opted for a natural method of contraception at some point in their life, making knowledge of the infertile period during the cycle

important for avoiding pregnancy. As the rhythm method is demonstrably unreliable, the ability to observe the mucus symptom which is a reliable indicator for periods of both infertility and fertility in a woman's cycle, becomes very important. All women in their reproductive years should at least have the option of learning to recognise and interpret their mucus symptom and have access to the self-understanding of their reproductive health and the predictability of their cycle.

In the US, Oklahoma City obstetrician-gynaecologist Dr Mary Martin, who was not always an advocate of natural family planning, became aware of the Billings Ovulation Method through her friendship with Suzanne Ek, the Executive Director of Billings Ovulation Method-USA. She believes that the teacher-training session she attended in St Cloud Minnesota in 2000 "profoundly changed how I approached gynaecology from that point on." Dr Martin confirmed the efficacy of the Method in treating infertility:

> Published data reveals that there is an 80% conception rate with the use of the Billings Ovulation Method. As I see 'problem' patients, by definition, simply identifying the fertile phase is not only essential, but results in the earliest possible pregnancy recognition in higher risk women. Moreover, the vast majority of women I see every day are anovulatory (they do not ovulate). The charting itself identifies anovulation while giving a clinical clue as to the underlying reason. I would have no career if the ovaries always performed as expected. There are only a handful of things which interfere with ovarian function. Identifying and treating these causes is infinitely rewarding.

Dr Martin said she did not prescribe contraception because of her religious views, but these were relevant to only a small minority of her patients.

> The truth about the underlying causes of anovulation is not a religious issue. Most who come to my practice do so because they want to know what their diagnosis is. If one ceases to prescribe contraceptives in a 'shotgun' approach to treating the gynaecologic maladies and actually investigates the underlying metabolic disturbance, patients become quite convinced when they see the results. An increasing number of evangelical Protestants are adopting natural family planning and eschewing unnatural means of infertility treatments.

In 2006, an independent report to the federal government estimated that about one in six Australian couples struggled with infertility. The question of how our medical expertise and resources should be allocated is complex and difficult. Given rising health care costs and limited resources, including those for assisted reproductive technology, it would be in Australia's interests to ensure that the benefits of inexpensive methods such as the BOM were promoted as a first step for couples struggling to conceive, before more intrusive and expensive options were explored.

It is also in the national interest to encourage solutions to sub-fertility and infertility. For every person aged 65 or older, Australia currently has five people in the paid workforce, a ratio that will halve to 2.5 workers as early as 2020 as the baby boomer generation ages and retires, precipitating a crisis in aged care.

The same applies around the world, including in Singapore, where former Prime Minister Lee Kuan Yew warned in August

2012 that his nation faced a demographic crisis, with the birth rate among Chinese Singaporeans falling to 1.08 children per woman, with 1.09 for Indians and 1.64 for Malays. Mr Lee, whose own government pushed for couples to "stop at two" children decades ago warned:

> If we go on like that, this place will fold up, because there'll be no original citizens left to form the majority, and we cannot have new citizens, new permanent residents to settle our social ethos, our social spirit, our social norms. So my message is a simple one.... we've got to persuade people to understand that getting married is important, having children is important. Do we want to replace ourselves or do we want to shrink and get older and be replaced by migrants and work permit holders? That's the simple question.

Wider testing of the BOM and other NFP methods would no doubt be required before they were widely adopted by mainstream fertility practices. By its nature, the Method could only help those women able to conceive by helping them identify the most fertile phase of their cycles. Economically it would make sense to at least explore the option, given the exorbitant rises in the cost of assisted reproductive technology and the growing demand. The report to the Howard Government on assisted reproductive technology showed that the number of ART services provided under Medicare rose from 131,000 for 19,000 patients in 2000 to 182,000 services for 27,000 patients in 2005. Over the same period, government spending on ART under Medicare and the Pharmaceutical Benefits Scheme more than doubled from $66 million in 2000 to $156 million in 2005. Analyses of Medicare figures showed that demand for ART procedures continued to escalate by about 10 per cent a year throughout the first decade of the 21st century.[3]

A slight slowdown was recorded, however, after concern over rising costs prompted the capping of Medicare benefits for ART procedures in 2010, by which time the cost of a cycle of IVF treatment had risen to $7000 to $8000.[4]

While overcoming infertility is, by popular demand, a principal focus of the BOM in Western nations, the WOOMB address to the UN spelled out how and why spacing or avoiding pregnancy remains the principal focus in the developing world. Susan Fryer told the General Assembly:

> The method is the most simple, natural and effective way in the world of achieving or avoiding pregnancy. In a 1978 five nation study, conducted by the World Health Organization, it was found that 93% of women can return, after just one conversation with a Billings teacher, with a recognisable chart of the few possibly fertile days and many infertile days in her cycle. With some further instruction in the keeping of a simple chart and in the application of a few common sense guidelines she will know on which days an act of intercourse can possibly lead to pregnancy and which ones that it cannot possibly do so, ahead of time. It allows parents to be in total charge of their fertility without the costly complications of the contraceptive /sterilization /abortion package ...
>
> I want to say a few words about the proven benefits of this method for mothers of families. It is their right to be told about it. There is now no doubt that the knowledge they acquire from it empowers them as they learn about the

physical changes that occur within their bodies. Women in developing nations report that the gift of knowledge of their own fertility enhances their self-esteem and status within their relationship and community. Understanding their own cycle gives them deeper insight into their womanhood and the dignity of being a woman. As well as that they will quickly learn to detect the development of abnormalities, so the Method proves to help women preserve gynaecological health.

Breast feeding women welcome the good news as it provides them with the security to resume sexual intercourse, without the worry of pregnancy, by accurately detecting the presence of their infertility while waiting for the return of their normal fertility. Women with irregular cycles learn to understand how they can use the knowledge. Mothers pass the information on to their daughters and parents welcome the knowledge that provides them with a healthy context in which to discuss fertility with their sons. Blind women are able to use the method as can women who have undergone the unnatural practice of female genital mutilation. Governments of over 100 nations appreciate the method as it provides them with the lowest cost policy option for fertility planning.[5]

If the telephones are quieter these days at the BOM Melbourne headquarters it is because much of the work, including teaching, is done online. More than 47,000 people visited the official Billings website, http://www.thebillingsovulationmethod.org/ from May 2011 to May 2012. While the largest numbers of Billings Ovulation Method users are in China and the developing world, visitors to the website over the past 12 months were predominantly from Australia (18,533), the United States

(11,547), Canada (3,459), the UK (2,143) as well as from the Philippines, Nigeria, Malaysia, India and France.

On the ground, WOOMB International works in conjunction with affiliate organisations as far afield as Brazil, Canada, Chile, China, Croatia, Cuba, Dominican Republic, Egypt, England, Ecuador, France, Hong Kong, Indonesia, Ireland, Italy, Kenya, Malaysia, Mexico, New Zealand, Pakistan, Peru, Poland, Scotland, Slovakia, Spain, Switzerland, Tanzania, Timor Leste, Uruguay the USA and Vietnam. In May 2011 Marie Marshell travelled to PNG to conduct planning and teaching workshops in Port Moresby in English and also in pidgin English with the help of an interpreter. For years, WOOMB's Darwin teachers have helped women in PNG learn the Method through correspondence courses.

Marie's visit coincided with a directive from the PNG Education Department ordering that condoms be supplied in schools to fight a soaring rate of HIV/AIDS. The Church in PNG announced it would not obey the directive because it contravened Catholic teaching on sexuality. Like all forms of NFP, the Billings Method, by its nature is not designed to prevent the spread of sexually transmitted diseases but is tied intrinsically to the concepts of chastity and fidelity, which are the surest means of preventing the spread of such diseases.

In 2012, Marie and Marian Corkill travelled to Peru and Cuba to conduct teacher training programs for BOM teachers. Despite the political difficulties, the Method has caught on in Cuba due to the long-time efforts of Dr Maria Concepcion Morales, a brave woman and the driving force behind Cuba's pro-life movement.

In Peru, the method is well-promoted by Dr Luis and Mrs Paulina Guisti who established a teaching organisation in Lima and by Canadian-born Maryknoll sister Josephina Lo Presti, a qualified nurse and teacher who worked for years in outlying areas of Peru and the northeast jungles of Bolivia and taught nursing at the Catholic University of Peru. Since the death of the Guistis and the retirement of Sister Josephina the work has continued to flourish thanks to the team of people they trained and inspired to take over.

1. http://www.finrrage.org/pdf_files/Newsletters/Newsletter_July_1999.pdf
2. *Bulletin of the Ovulation Method Research and Reference Centre of Australia*, November 2009.
3. http://www.health.gov.au/internet/main/publishing.nsf/Content/356F66F51D5D4163CA2571F50009EE7B/$File/artrc_report.pdf
4. http://www.smh.com.au/national/health/women-put-off-ivf-after-costs-rise-20111025-1mi5i.html
5. UN speech, http://www.finrrage.org/pdf_files/Newsletters/Newsletter_July_1999.pdf

John addressing Pope John Paul II

Drs Billings with Pope John Paul II in 1987

9

The BOM and the Sensus Fidelium

After lying almost dormant for decades, a series of recent controversies over the Catholic Church's opposition to artificial birth control has rekindled interest and passions on both sides of a debate that was never properly resolved in the minds of many people.

In 2010, the row that erupted in the United States when the Obama administration attempted to introduce healthcare changes under which "preventive services" including contraception and sterilisation would be included in all health insurance plans, showed that the Church's teaching retained the potential to spark controversy.

US Catholic bishops said that they would not support the Obama administration's proposed compromise on a controversial rule that requires most employers to fully cover contraception in their workers' health plans. In a controversy that continued throughout 2012, the US Conference of Catholic Bishops, which had led opposition to the proposal, also rejected a compromise under which employers who objected to the use of contraception would have had the right to exclude it from their policies, although employees who wanted it would have been able to obtain it from the relevant insurance companies.[1] For many young Catholics, the row was the first indication they had received of the significance of the issue in the Church's moral theology.

In mid-2012, the US Catholic bishops began promoting natural family planning more pro-actively than before. Bishop Kevin C. Rhoades of the Diocese of Fort Wayne-South Bend, Indiana, who chairs the Committee on Laity, Marriage, Family Life, and Youth of the US Conference of Catholic Bishops admitted: "Sadly, the majority of Catholics still do not know about Church teachings on married love nor understand why the Church considers artificial contraception immoral. This, tragically, is due to inconsistent education and formation since 1968. Over the last 30 years, we have been striving to correct the situation."

Cardinal Timothy Dolan, the Archbishop of New York, was even more blunt in March 2012. Reported in the *Wall Street Journal,* he said *Humanae Vitae* "brought such a tsunami of dissent, departure, disapproval of the Church, that I think most of us — and I'm using the first-person plural intentionally, including myself — kind of subconsciously said, 'Whoa. We'd better never talk about that, because it's just too hot to handle'."

In doing so "we forfeited the chance to be a coherent moral voice when it comes to one of the more burning issues of the day." Sex abuse scandals, he said, "intensified our laryngitis over speaking about issues of chastity and sexual morality, because we almost thought, 'I'll blush if I do ... After what some priests and some bishops, albeit a tiny minority, have done, how will I have any credibility in speaking on that?'"

But, Cardinal Dolan added, Catholic youth were "now

demanding that the Church speak authoritatively on issues of sexuality. They will be quick to say, 'By the way, we want you to know that we might not be able to obey it ... But we want to hear it. And in justice, you as our pastors need to tell us, and you need to challenge us'."

There is no doubt that natural family planning and *Humanae Vitae* have had a rough passage over their first four decades, their acceptance impeded by the trends of the times, poor explanation and teaching within the Church and its institutions including schools and by confusion and sometimes conflicting attitudes and medical approaches.

But nor has the alternative, contraception, enjoyed a smooth or enviable record. Surely the biggest failure of the various methods is to be found in the fact that Australian taxpayers fund more than 70,000 abortions annually through Medicare. Reliability of barrier methods is a major concern, as are the side-effects, immediate and long term, of the Pill and the IUD. Given the efficacy of the Billings Ovulation Method in successive surveys around the world, it is fair to conclude that Dr Thomas Hilgers was correct when he said the "full potential" of the ovulation method is yet to be achieved. Whether or not it is achieved in the foreseeable future will depend on numerous, complex factors within society, the Catholic Church and developments within the medical profession.

Controversy also flared in 2012 over a campaign launched by practising Catholic and philanthropist Melinda Gates to distribute contraceptives to African women. On 31 July 2012, the Vatican's *L'Osservatore Romano* newspaper published an article by Italian journalist Giulia Galeotti attacking Mrs Gates's campaign and questioning why she was not more aware of the Billings Ovulation Method.

"An example, little known but striking, of the success of BOM has been its adoption in China," Galeotti wrote. "The communist government of Peking was very interested in a method of regulation that cost nothing and didn't damage the health of the woman, a method considered 98% reliable."

The "original and unpardonable sin," of the BOM, she said, was that " it is completely free, an aspect that, evidently, makes it very unpopular with the pharmaceutical industry, which, through chemical contraceptives, obtains enormous profits, as will others thanks to the philanthropy of Mrs. Gates."

Earlier in July, in an interview with *The Guardian* newspaper in London, Mrs Gates said she had agonised over whether to speak out in defiance of the Church hierarchy. "Of course I wrestled with this. As a Catholic I believe in this religion, there are amazing things about this religion, amazing moral teachings that I do believe in, but I also have to think about how we keep women alive. I believe in not letting women die, I believe in not letting babies die, and to me that's more important than arguing about what method of contraception [is right]."

Gates, who was attending the London Summit on Family Planning organised by her foundation in association with the British Government and the United Nations Population Fund (UNFPA), said that since she had announced her initiative a few weeks earlier she had been inundated with messages of support from Catholic women, including nuns.

"A church is made up of its members, and one of the things this campaign might do is help women speak out. I've had thousands of women come on to websites and say 'I'm a Catholic, but I believe in contraception.' It's going to be women voting with their feet," she said. "In my country 82% of Catholics say contraception is morally acceptable. So let the women in Africa decide. The choice is up to them."[2] Later that year the UN declared access to contraception to be a basic human right.

To a large extent, the question of whether the Billings Ovulation Method ever becomes mainstream among Catholics in Australia and other Western societies will depend on several factors. These include attitudes within the medical profession and broader community towards sexual morality and marriage. For all the empirical evidence about its effectiveness, there is no doubt that the Ovulation Method will only work for women in committed, stable relationships with a partner who is willing to take responsibility for their fertility as a couple. By its nature, it has little or nothing to offer women pursuing casual sexual relationships, or their partners. It is equally problematic for married women whose husbands refuse to co-operate.

Basically, while pinpointing the woman's fertile days, the Method requires abstinence for about 14 days of a 28-day cycle (including the days of menstruation) for couples wanting to avoid conception. As the Mayo Clinic website advises, the Method requires "motivation and diligence".

But is such a discipline realistic? Over time, adherents of the Method have reported a long-term heightened satisfaction in their relationships and less taking each other for granted. Nor are its strictures wildly at odds with the reality of many couples' lives. La Trobe University's 2001-2002 Australian Study of Health and Relationships survey of more than 19,300 adult Australians reported that most people had sex less than twice a week. "Those who had been in heterosexual relationships for at least twelve months had sex on average 1.84 times a week in the past four weeks, with younger people having sex more frequently."

One factor likely to affect the future of all forms of natural family planning is attitudes within the Catholic hierarchy and how they filter down to people in the pews. In a potted survey of 12 orthodox priests in three states prepared for this book, who ranged in age from their mid-20s to their early 80s, all admitted that the issue of contraception was "rarely if ever" mentioned to them in the confessional. Several, however, said that when it was raised it had the potential to cause anxiety. Most of the priests said it was more common to be approached by infertile couples who were anxious about the use of IVF and other procedures forbidden by the Church, mainly because they involved the creation of numerous embryos that were ultimately destroyed. All agreed that in their experience, the Billings Method and Dr Hilgers' NaProTECHNOLOGY had much to offer couples struggling to conceive.

As to the issue of whether the Church can indefinitely maintain such a significant teaching that is so widely disregarded Bishop Fisher responded:

> No part of the Catholic faith is a dead letter, even if it is lived very imperfectly and rarely talked about in a particular period in history. I know many faithful married

couples who do not use artificial contraception and welcome children lovingly into their homes. I know many who have been helped by John and Lyn Billings or their associates over the past few decades. Quietly, humbly and guided by the Holy Spirit, the Church and many of her members will remain faithful to the Lord's call to welcome new life as the participation in His creative work.

While the Catholic Church's moral teaching on contraception remains outside the orbit of many young Catholics, an event in Sydney in May 2011 suggests that at a sizeable minority are open to it and keenly interested. The popular youth forum, Theology on Tap, regularly draws hundreds of young people to hear thought-provoking speakers. It attracted its largest-ever crowd when Jason Evert from the US, a staff apologist with Catholic Answers, a non-profit organisation dedicated to promoting the Catholic faith through all forms of media, spoke about "Contraception versus Natural Family Planning" in a talk entitled "Green Sex; All Natural & All Good". Theology on Tap co-ordinator Jessica Langrell said members of the crowd _ especially those thinking of getting married in the foreseeable future – were deeply interested both in the teaching and practicalities of natural family planning.

One leading academic who was not surprised by such interest on the part of young people is Professor Tracey Rowland, the Dean of the John Paul II Institute for Marriage and the Family in Melbourne. In "The Wars of Love: A Review of Fergus Kerr's *Twentieth Century Catholic Theologians*", published in the *Josephinum Journal of Theology* in 2011, Professor Rowland expressed the hope that "an unsensationalised nuptial mysticism will form the foundation of a renaissance of Catholic family life in the next two to three generations". As she pointed out:

> Certainly there are thousands of youth worldwide who are currently studying John Paul II's theology of the body and the nuptial mysticism of Cardinals Angelo Scola and Marc Ouellet. Many of them are at one of the international network of John Paul II Institutes. At the very least the current generation of Catholic youth will have had the best opportunities to study the theology of marriage of any generation in history. The generation of '68 had only marriage manuals in the language of marital dues and contract law and a couple of encyclicals in which even Ratzinger has acknowledged 'the theology was rather slim'. Given this, and the anti-large family practices of the western economic order, it is no wonder that a couple of generations found the teaching difficult and even incomprehensible.[3]

Aware of the difficulties and of the centrality of the Church teachings on marriage and the family to Catholics' lives, Pope John Paul II established a series of institutes for the study of marriage and the family around the world. The Pope was on his way to open the Roman headquarters of the Institute, at the Pontifical Lateran University in Rome on 13 May 1981 when he was gunned down by Turkish terrorist Ali Agca, whose bullet came within a whisker of taking the Pope's life. Since that time the Institute has operated under the patronage of Our Lady of Fatima.

The idea for the Institutes, Professor Rowland said, arose as a result of the young Bishop Karol Wojtyla's pastoral experience in Krakow under communism, when financial, bureaucratic and social pressures on families were intense:

Cardinal Wojtyła understood that alcoholism and domestic violence are usually symptoms of other underlying problems and thus it was futile to simply remind married couples of their duties and to deliver homilies against bad behaviour. If the family was to survive and indeed flourish as a social organism it needed infrastructural support. The Church's pastors needed to understand the pressure being exerted by the culture in which people worked and lived.

Cardinal Wojtyła also understood that the Church needed to develop a theology of marriage that went beyond the formulae of the neo-scholastic marriage manuals which were widely used before the Second Vatican Council.

He wanted to inject some of the insights from personalist philosophy into the Church's teaching in this area. In other

Lyn and John with Pope John Paul II in 1987

words, he wanted to draw into the Church's theology of marriage ideas which are now presented to the world under the label of "Lublin Thomism".

As Professor Rowland pointed out, John Paul II's highly personalist account of the meaning of sexuality appealed to many young people. This included the millions who encountered it around the world on his extensive travels, and especially at the World Youth Days he instigated:

> It offered them an alternative to the pragmatic attitude of the previous two generations," Professor Rowland wrote. "For this generation, being told that in the act of love they are participating in the life of the Trinity, and that their bodies are nothing less than 'radiant icons of Trinitarian processions' sounds like a much more noble reason to live in poverty and trust in providence, than references to violations of the natural moral law which are likely to be confused with the notion of natural fertility rhythms.
>
> This is also a generation which is more sceptical of technological solutions than its parents, and for whom 'organic is good' and chemical intervention is bad. Once the word gets out that the contraceptive Pill is linked to a loss of libido (because of the suppression of estrogen) and feminists start writing articles against pharmaceutical companies, the magisterial teaching may start to look more avant-garde than old-fashioned.
>
> Already there is a growing convergence of radical feminism and John Paul II Catholicism on the plane of biotechnology. Feminists are critical of the treatment of women as commodities and machines.
>
> Leaving aside such pragmatic social developments, the point is simply that the current generation is faced with

a dominant account of sexuality which runs something like this: sex can be for fun or it can be for reproduction. You are expected to be sexually active for fun from your early teenage years up to your late twenties or early thirties when your intentions might change to reproduction. During the fun period it is important to protect yourself from pregnancy by using contraceptives, and to protect yourself from sexually transmitted diseases by insisting that your partner uses a condom. When you are ready to reproduce you should go through some kind of marriage ceremony primarily for the legal and financial benefits. You then resume the use of contraceptives after you have had two children or three if you are having trouble getting one of each.

For the current generation of youth for whom this or something like it appears as the dominant social attitude, sexuality is largely recreational, mechanical and mundane. Magazines for teenage girls include such special features as 'the sexual position of the month' with technicolour details of how to achieve the position. Sex is no longer draped in mystery and when mystery goes so too does sacrality. In this picture there is little room for romance, chivalry or what was once called courtship. Moreover, there is no place for the theo-dramatic. Sex has no cosmic significance. It is all so banal. However this is precisely one of the reasons why John Paul II appealed to young people. He restored to sex its cosmic significance and to young people their dignity. He could only do it by going back to theological basics and explaining what it means to be made in the image of God. Significantly, it was not some kind of merely theistically coloured God, some first cause, but the explicitly Trinitarian God described in the personalist language of relationships. Moreover, the nuptial mystery theology places an accent on the greatness of marriage and family life, it makes having a family sound like an adventure for talented people, rather than something that only social losers do.

It remains to be seen how the issue plays out in coming decades. It would be unthinkable that the Church would ever approve any form of contraception that destroyed life, even at its earliest stages, such as the IUD. Some Catholics, however, see scope for a revision of the issue in which the sanctity of life was central, with decisions on other matters, such as NFP, barrier methods, or other non-abortifacient contraception, left to individuals. Any change to the Church's fundamental opposition to contraception, however, would appear highly unlikely although a minimalist

John and Lyn with Pope Benedict XVI in 2005

approach, within strict limits that protected life from the moment of conception, would have its advantages. Indeed, it was Pope Benedict XVI himself who startled supporters and critics alike in 2010 when he raised the issue of condoms in preventing the spread of AIDS. In an interview with his biographer, German journalist Peter Seewald for *Light of the World*, published by Ignatius Press, the Pope acknowledged:

> There may be a basis in the case of some individuals, as perhaps when a male prostitute uses a condom, where this can be a first step in the direction of a moralization, a first assumption of responsibility, on the way toward recovering an awareness that not everything is allowed and that one cannot do whatever one wants. But it is not really the way to deal with the evil of HIV infection. That can really lie only in a humanization of sexuality.

The Pope was then asked by Seewald: "Are you saying, then, that the Catholic Church is actually not opposed in principle to the use of condoms?"

Benedict replied: "She of course does not regard it as a real or moral solution, but, in this or that case, there can be nonetheless, in the intention of reducing the risk of infection, a first step in a movement toward a different way, a more human way, of living sexuality."

The Pope's answer, while directed towards curbing the spread of AIDS, set some people wondering whether, at some future time, the door might be opened officially to the use of condoms for preventing conception, perhaps in conjunction with natural family planning. Professor Rowland, for one, who has studied the theology of Benedict XVI in depth for years is certain that the Church would never countenance the separation of the procreative and unitive functions of marriage by condoning contraception. This is spelt out clearly in the *Catechism of the Catholic Church*, revised in the early 1980s. It states:

> For just reasons, spouses may wish to space the births of their children. It is their duty to make certain that their desire is not motivated by selfishness but is in conformity with the generosity appropriate to responsible parenthood. Moreover, they should conform their behaviour to the objective criteria of morality (2368).
>
> By safeguarding both these essential aspects, the unitive and the procreative, the conjugal act preserves in its fullness the sense of true mutual love and its orientation toward man's exalted vocation to parenthood (2369).
>
> Periodic continence, that is, the methods of birth regulation based on self-observation and the use of infertile periods, is in conformity with the objective criteria of morality. These methods respect the bodies of the spouses, encourage tenderness between them, and favour the education of an authentic freedom. In contrast, "every action which, whether in anticipation of the conjugal act, or in its accomplishment, or in the development of its natural consequences, proposes, whether as an end or as a means, to render procreation impossible" is intrinsically evil:
>
> Thus the innate language that expresses the total reciprocal self-giving of husband and wife is overlaid, through contraception, by an objectively contradictory language, namely, that of not giving oneself totally to the other. This leads not only to a positive refusal to be open to life but also to a falsification of the inner truth of conjugal love,

which is called upon to give itself in personal totality.... the difference, both anthropological and moral, between contraception and recourse to the rhythm of the cycle . . . involves in the final analysis two irreconcilable concepts of the human person and of human sexuality (2370).

Let all be convinced that human life and the duty of transmitting it are not limited by the horizons of this life only: their true evaluation and full significance can be understood only in reference to man's eternal destiny (2371).

In an address to scholars of the University of Lublin in April 2012 on John Paul II – Pope of the civilisation of love – Professor Rowland explained the central place of the Church's teaching on marriage in terms of God's creation:

> John Paul II's *Catechesis on Human Love*, delivered as a series of Wednesday audience addresses in the early years of his pontificate, anthropology was linked to Trinitarian theology and sexuality was situated within this framework of God's offer of divine filiation. Within this *katological* framework (working downwards from the Trinity to the person), the married couple is raised to the exalted position of being a 'radiant icon of Trinitarian love' and the seal of their marital holiness is viewed as nothing less than a 'supernatural work of art' ...
>
> In treating sexuality in this context John Paul II brought to an end the reign of neo-scholastic marriage manuals with their emphasis on rights and duties, and in their place he forged a new theological path in the Catholic understanding of the meaning and purpose of human sexuality. This path or approach is now described by theologians as 'nuptial mysticism'. It is all a million miles from the idea that marriage is a remedy for concupiscence and other

unhelpful ideas which entered into the mainstream of Catholic attitudes to sexuality via the Jansenist heresy.[4]

Various aspects of the debate will contiue, however. In the lead-up to the 2013 Conclave, German Cardinal Joachim Meisner of Cologne, a long-time friend of Benedict XVI, raised an interesting dilemma when he apologised after two Catholic hospitals refused to admit a 25-year-old woman who believed she had been drugged and possibly raped at a party. Doctors said the hospitals refused to admit the woman because the prescribed course of treatment would involve using the morning-after pill. Amid strong public reaction, Meisner said that if "a medication that hinders conception is used after a rape with the purpose of avoiding fertilisation, then this is acceptable in my view".

Critics, however, including the president of the World Federation of Catholic Medical Associations, Jose Maria Simon Castellvi, argued that manufacturers of the morning-after pill said the drug might prevent an embryo from implanting on the uterine wall and therefore "we cannot accept it, since even a microscopic human embryo is a person with rights, dignity and a son of God".

Balancing compassion for those under pressure with the importance of protecting life from the moment of conception will remain an ongoing challenge in promoting the culture of life.

Only on one significant and complex moral issue – the continuation of "artificial" feeding and hydration for people in a persistent vegetative state – did John Billings' professional views clash publicly with official Church opinion. The case that brought his views into the open was one that sparked passionate debate among doctors, politicians, church leaders, pro-life and euthanasia advocates. It centred on a 69-year-old woman as "Mrs BWV" who died in Victoria in June 2003. The woman, who had suffered from a form of dementia known as Pick's Disease, was taken off artificial life support, in accordance with her husband's and family's wishes, after the Supreme Court ruled that the tube was medical rather than palliative treatment and could therefore be legally withdrawn. The woman died just over three weeks after the court order was made.

For various reasons, the case triggered intense responses, with the Victorian Voluntary Euthanasia Society president Rodney Symes arguing at the time that the circumstances surrounding Mrs BWV's death strengthened the case for voluntary euthanasia by lethal injection. "You've got to ask the question: Is it in the best interests of BWV to have died of dehydration over a three-week period?" he told the Herald Sun. "There is no dignity in a slow death by dehydration and starvation."

At the opposite end of the spectrum, the Catholic Church and Right to Life Australia, which had both made submissions to the Supreme Court arguing against removal of the feeding tube, warned that the judgement would place vulnerable people at risk. The then-Director of the John Paul II Institute for Marriage and the Family in Melbourne, Father Anthony Fisher, said the prospect of tube feeding being removed "from the unconscious or the demented or the mentally handicapped" was "a very serious matter."

John Billings had a different view, however, in relation to Mrs BWV's case, arguing in the National Civic Council publication,

News Weekly, in May 2003 that removing the feeding tube was not a form of euthanasia but allowing nature to take its course.

While his arguments prompted widespread dismay in Catholic circles, many found them convincing. He wrote:

> Before any evidence of the onset of Pick's Disease, the patient and her husband had discussed together and sometimes with the two eldest daughters, as to whether they would want their lives to be prolonged if they ever developed incapacity; they all expressed the opinion that they would not wish to live any longer if such serious disability ever occurred.
>
> The husband and all six children now support the idea that the mother should be allowed to die, although one son mentioned that if he thought that his mother could get better (which is impossible) he would have a different view....
>
> Because she is unable to swallow any food or fluid given by mouth, she is doubly incontinent, that is of bladder and bowels, and spontaneous emptying of these organs occurs through the action of spinal reflexes.
>
> As a result the patient now requires to be moved by a hoist to the shower and after cleaning there is an application of pads, to protect her skin as far as possible.
>
> She requires regular avoidance of pressure, having previously developed some pressure ulcers which were healed as a result of the excellent care she had received in the hospital; they remain a threat of recurrence as a result of her continuing deterioration. She has no cognitive capacity at all and appears to be unable to appreciate any painful stimuli. She is incapable of any movement but will follow with her eyes anyone who comes to her bedside.
>
> There is no treatment known that has any curative

influence upon the progressive deterioration which occurs in Pick's Disease until the patient dies. The performance of the operation and the continual use of the aperture made in the abdominal wall to deliver nourishment and sedatives to the stomach takes the treatment beyond the range of what is called Palliative Care.

This was clearly understood by all those who participated in the discussions regarding management of the present situation, just as it was as clearly understood that the discussions were in no way a consideration of euthanasia.

Withdrawing burdensome treatment which has no useful influence upon an incurable disease is not euthanasia. Discussions have now occurred between this devoted husband and a public advocate regarding a guardianship order with respect to the patient, and the husband stated that he would be agreeable to this authority being given to the public advocate as they had found that their opinions were in agreement, each with the other. If the nutrition and fluid administration were discontinued, the mild sedation could be continued and it is unlikely that the woman would be conscious of any serious discomfort.

The valid conclusion to be made is clearly that which the woman had made many years ago and with which all the members of the family now agree, that it would be a mercy to release her from her undignified and grave incapacity by discontinuing the tube feeding and allowing her to die.

John also had a letter published on the matter in Melbourne's *Herald Sun* newspaper, arguing: "It needs to be clearly understood that when an individual is totally incapacitated by an incurable illness, it is not morally wrong to withdraw futile treatment that is doing nothing more than prolonging the natural progress that forms the terminal stage of the illness ..."[5]

However convincing many would find such arguments, the Vatican did not. Mrs BWV's case aroused the interest of doctors, ethicists and theologians throughout the world, including those at the highest levels in the Church.

In an address to an International Congress, "Life-Sustaining Treatments and Vegetative State: Scientific Advances and Ethical Dilemmas" on 20 March 2004, Pope John Paul II gave an authoritative response on what remains a difficult and sensitive subject:

> The sick person in a vegetative state, awaiting recovery or a natural end, still has the right to basic health care (nutrition, hydration, cleanliness, warmth, etc.), and to the prevention of complications related to his confinement to

John and Lyn with members of their family after receipt of the Order of Australia medals

bed. He also has the right to appropriate rehabilitative care and to be monitored for clinical signs of eventual recovery.

I should like particularly to underline how the administration of water and food, even when provided by artificial means, always represents a *natural means* of preserving life, not a *medical act*. Its use, furthermore, should be considered, in principle, *ordinary* and *proportionate*, and as such morally obligatory, insofar as and until it is seen to have attained its proper finality, which in the present case consists in providing nourishment to the patient and alleviation of his suffering.[6]

Overwhelmingly, however, the Billings' thinking and legacy, were at one with the approach of Pope John Paul II. The late Holy Father personally added a star to John's papal knighthood in 2003, the year in which he also named Evelyn as a Papal Dame of St Gregory the Great.

In her meetings with Paul VI, John Paul II and Benedict XVI, Evelyn found that all three were well acquainted with hers and John's work and appreciative of it. From 1980, Evelyn served the Vatican as a member of the Pontifical Council for Life, which John Paul II established and which comprises theologians, bishops and lay people to advise the Church on developing the culture of life that the late Pontiff called for in *Evangelium Vitae*.

On a visit to Rome for two conferences in February and March 1998, they were among the delegates who met Pope John Paul II, whom Lyn recalled was "walking slowly" after surgical treatment for a fractured hip but was good humoured and alert. "As soon as he approached us he called us by name and thanked us for our work ...". Pressing a Rosary into each of their hands, he expressed great interest and a thorough knowledge of their work in China.

John and Evelyn were also thrilled when their work was recognised officially by their homeland in 1991 when they were appointed Members of the Order of Australia. As Evelyn told the *Herald Sun* on Australia Day 1996 they were especially pleased that the award was offered to both of them "because it really has been a partnership - we've been married for 48 years and for more than half that time we have been working on this (Method)."[7]

Perhaps the ultimate significance of their work, however, is best summed up by one of John's favourite Old Testament passages. Writing in his diary, he applied it to the "good missionary people" and "the people they love so much and serve so well" whom he encountered in India in January 1983:

"The learned will shine with the brilliance of the firmament, and those who train many in the ways of justice will sparkle like the stars for all eternity" (Daniel 12:3).

1. *Wall Street Journal*, 12 February 2012.
2. http://www.guardian.co.uk/world/2012/jul/11/melinda-gates-challenges-vatican-contraception
3. Tracey Rowland. "The Wars of Love: A Review of Fergus Kerr's *Twentieth Century Catholic Theologians*", *Josephinum Journal of Theology,* 2011.
4. Tracey Rowland. "John Paul II – Pope of the civilisation of love". Address at Lublin University, 2 April 2012.
5. "Tube woman can die court rules landmark decision", *The Age*, 30 May 2003, p. 5.
6. *Herald Sun*, 19 January 2003, p. 26.
7. http://www.vatican.va/holy_father/john_paul_ii/speeches/2004/march/documents/hf_jp-ii_spe_20040320_congress-fiamc_en.html
8. *Herald Sun*, 26 January 1991.

Outside St Patrick's Cathedral, Melbourne, after receiving their Papal awards from Archbishop Denis Hart in 2003

Drs Evelyn and John Billings

Epilogue

Requiem Mass for the soul of Evelyn Billings was celebrated at St Patrick's Cathedral on Thursday, 21 February 2013. Her family chose the first reading from the book of Proverbs and it could not have been more apt: "A perfect wife – who can find her? She is far beyond the price of pearls. Her husband's heart has confidence in her, from her he will derive no little profit."

Evelyn herself had chosen the Gospel as well as the Second Reading from the first letter of St John, about the love of God.

"Not our love of God, but God's love for us," as Father Jerome Santamaria, grand-nephew of the Billings' old friend Dr Joe Santamaria said in his homily.

"Once we realise how much we are loved by God, we cannot but respond. As the motto of St Vincent's reads: *Caritas Christi urget nos*. The love of Christ impels us. Once we have tasted true life, there is no going back. And when we respond, we cannot settle for anything else but a total response. We must be true to the love we know."

The Mass highlighted the love that underpinned this extraordinary woman's life. A tribute printed in the Mass booklet from her Canadian friend, Father Joseph Hattie OMI, spoke of some of the labours of Evelyn's love that continue to bear fruit that will last: "The story of how the seeds of truth were lovingly planted in India by Dr Lyn teaching the Method to Blessed Mother Teresa's nuns for the benefit of the poor in Calcutta; or the story of how she taught the first 20 women obstetricians/gynaecologists in China."

Dr John and Lyn were famous, the tribute continued, a fame of which many of their grandchildren were not aware. In 2005, when they were awarded honorary Doctorates of Medicine at Tor Vegata University in Rome, two of their granddaughters, working in Europe at the time, came for the occasion "and were amazed at how famous their grandparents were."

Perhaps that was a good sign. As Father Hattie said: "Humility, which according to St Teresa of Avila is truth, is essential for a person called by God to bear the enormous amount of fruit He asked of her and John. She had that humility and always recognised that it was God's work and that she, with John, were merely His instruments of peace."

In their tributes, Lyn's sons Jimmy and Peter depicted a woman at ease with herself and the world and who relished every stage of her long, rich life. Peter reminded the congregation of Lyn's childhood in Jerilderie, and the horses, dogs, cats and wildlife she had loved and told him about.

> The things I liked hearing about were her father's passions: duck and quail and snipe shooting, catching enormous Murray cod in the Billabong Creek, fly fishing on the Mitta Mitta River for brown trout, and sea fishing at Durras Waters near Bateman's Bay where he would catch whopping flathead. These stories fired my imagination and kindled the desire to do such things myself.
>
> And I always looked forward to telling her about my adventures – and she loved to listen. I remember well in

my 20s and 30s studying the psychology of personality and learning about people who reach the pinnacle of mental health. They had certain characteristics – they accepted themselves as they were, were accepting and not judgemental of others, were open to change, creative and spontaneous and often humorous and spiritually alive. They tended to be unsentimental, flexible and not given to sarcasm or superiority. I began to realise that I knew someone like this – my mother.

Jimmy recounted a story that his mother wanted told:

> It's a school morning. We are summoned to breakfast by a banging on an old gun shell in the kitchen. As we sit around the huge oblong laminex table there is Honey (Lyn), the porridge
>
> pot gurgling away on the stove, tomatoes and toast ready for the customary cooked breakfast, and Honey making cut lunches for us all. Can you picture all those sandwiches, pieces of cake, fruit, grease proof paper, brown paper bags for the mob of children. Then she'd get us out the door, clean up the considerable debris, get herself ready and then off she'd go in her FX Holden to be a doctor.

He also spoke of Lyn's parents – his grandmother "Wudda" who had a "delicious sense of humour which she passed on to her daughter" and his grandfather, "Jerilderie Pop", who encouraged Lyn to be a doctor. "Mother often spoke fondly of her school life in Jerilderie. Although the Principal was a bit of a rogue keeping a bottle of whisky at the ready behind the piano. He often took his charges for ramblings in the bush sharing his love of nature and sitting them under a gum tree and reading stories and poetry."

Life was harder and lonelier for Lyn living with her grandparents in Melbourne to attend secondary school. "Music saved her. When things were tough she would often retreat to the Music Room and play the piano." Jimmy also revealed the real story of his parents' romance, how John Billings had noticed "this lovely young lady and told his friends he would like to meet her" before he encountered her in the dissecting room of the medical school. But turbulence lay ahead:

> A devout Catholic falling in love with a devout Anglican. A world where animosity often existed between the denominations. Where members of each flock had been taught to separate themselves from the other.
>
> Well love conquers all, they say. Mother did tell me though that at one stage she did write Dad a "Dear John" letter (literally) saying she wanted to end it. Whether it was an inefficient Jerilderie postal service or Divine Intervention the letter never arrived. There was Dad waiting as he always did to meet her at Spencer Street Railway Station with a bunch of flowers … the letter was never mentioned!
>
> After careful thought, prayer and meditation mother converted to the Catholic Church. She often told us how much she had gained from doing this. We have watched her undying faith strengthen and sustain her throughout her life. She has been an extraordinary servant of the Catholic Church. This is well documented. AND she has taught many Catholics to love Anglicans!

On behalf of her fellow Directors of WOOMB International – Joan Clements, Kerry Bourke and Marian Corkill – Marie Marshell spoke of Lyn in terms of what Pope John Paul II called "the feminine genius", a genius for relationships between persons, whether human or divine.

> Lyn once said that you really get to know someone when you travel with them. I speak today as one of the Billings teachers who has been blessed with spending long periods of time in her company. I have witnessed her warmth and generosity to the poorest of the poor. I have seen her unfailing courtesy when sorely tested by the difficulties and privations of travel as she, with John, continued to carry out the work entrusted to them by the Lord. I have seen her joy and pride in John and seen his gentle and unfailing care for her.
>
> I heard her chuckles at life's small foibles as we strung our washing to dry across our bedroom windows and her laughter as she shared pieces of a petticoat torn to be used as a cleaning cloth. We enjoyed our little cup of whisky and water, and sometimes Aussie cheese and biscuits carried all the way from home, as we came together for that special hour after a long day to share the triumphs and challenges we had each encountered. They were precious times of laughter and John jokes.
>
> One image that stays with me happened many years ago, travelling through the winter darkness somewhere in the Anwei province of China after a long, long day of arduous travel in an old and uncomfortable van, accompanied by various officials. We sang songs until we were all exhausted and I saw Lyn's head falling gently onto John's chest. For the rest of the long and bumpy ride he sat holding her firmly and she rested easily in his arms. I saw how uncomfortable he had to be to continue without moving for the next hour or so. I witnessed pure love and

the beauty of their relationship worked its own magic on many of the people with whom we worked.

Through our years of travel, I have also been allowed to know the loving wife, mother, grandmother and great-grandmother. I have prayed with Lyn, shared in the sadness of anniversaries of their beloved Ruth, heard of the wonderful accomplishments of grandchildren and witnessed the joy at the birth of each new member of the large Billings clan. I saw how precious these little ones were in Lyn's eyes and I understood why the work she was called to do, to be an instrument of peace in a world which sees a threat in the very existence of these precious small ones, could not be put aside.

Lyn's dear friend Bishop Peter Elliott spoke briefly before the final prayers of commendation. He mentioned the motto of WOOMB International chosen by John and Lyn – *Credidimus caritati*: We have put our faith in love – saying how very appropriate the motto was not only for the life of these two remarkable doctors but also for those who continue their work. He also voiced what many in the congregation and others around the world had thought and said in the days since Lyn's death – the hope that the Church will in time recognise this couple as Blessed as they are surely already known in heaven.

As the moving notes of *In Paradisium* faded, Lyn's family – her eight living children and their spouses, her 39 grandchildren and their spouses and her 31 great-grandchildren – filled the aisle of the great Cathedral as they moved outside into the warm summer noon. There, under the leafy green of great trees planted generations ago, as the Collins Street trams clattered past en route to Kew and the areas that the Billings knew and loved, the youngest children – the next generation – released their pent up energies. In high spirits they dashed around the Pilgrim Path, water features and among the sculptures of the great and good around the Cathedral grounds.

Daniel O'Connell, Daniel Mannix, Saint Mary MacKillop and a range of saints official and unofficial ... they might even sit comfortably, one day, alongside an additional sculpture of a husband and wife with stethoscopes around their necks, who made their marks, for overwhelming good, in Melbourne, nationally, and around the world.

Acknowledgements

The Billings Enigma came together into a coherent whole with a lot of help from some very good, deeply committed people. I was extremely fortunate, early on in the project, to have the chance to interview the inestimable Dr Evelyn Billings in her living room at home in Kew. It was a memorable encounter. If ever a couple deserved a book about their lives and achievements it is Lyn and her late husband, John. I am also grateful to their son, David Billings, for sharing his memories of his parents and to their daughter, Eve Provan, for doing the same and for rounding up and copying precious family photographs.

Thank you, also, to Joan Clements, Director of WOOMB International Ltd, for commissioning me to write this book then managing to remain both hands-off and co-operative throughout. One of our few areas of disagreement was over the use of the comma. Joan is a fan, I like to keep them to a minimum, so we compromised! The assistance and insights of Marian Corkill, Director, WOOMB International Ltd; Marie Marshell, Director, WOOMB International Ltd and Merilyn Kennealy, Archivist of the organisation, were invaluable. It was a privilege and a great help to be able to read Dr John Billings' diaries of his many forays overseas.

Cardinal George Pell, with a dollop of wisdom and a dash of wit, provided a splendid foreword for which I am most grateful. I am also indebted to Australia's leading bioethicist, Bishop Anthony Fisher of Parramatta, for taking time to answer a long list of questions in writing, as did Dr Thomas Hilgers MD, director of the Pope Paul VI Institute for the Study of Human Reproduction in Omaha, Nebraska.

Grateful thanks to Professor Tracey Rowland for her fascinating and brilliant theological insights. This work owes much to John and Lyn's dear friends Bishop Peter Elliott and Dr Joe Santamaria for sharing their recollections and ideas so generously. The Medical insights of Dr Mary Walsh in Melbourne and Dr Mary Martin in the US were also vital.

I also thank Kerry Bourke, Director, WOOMB International Ltd, Father Peter Joseph and members of the Billings family for doing such a thorough job as proof-readers; Matthew, Rosanne and Lachlan Rose for their hospitality in Melbourne and Anthony and Brigid Cappello for their intellectual and entrepreneurial flair in operating Connor Court Publishing.

And as always in writing about the big questions of life, I was guided by the faith that Fr Tim Norris PP has instilled in me and tens of thousands of his parishioners over his remarkable, 57-year career in the service of Our Lord.

www.ingramcontent.com/pod-product-compliance
Lightning Source LLC
Chambersburg PA
CBHW070807230426
43665CB00017B/2520